When Chang-di 'Robin' Yeh departed on his scheduled recon flight on November 1, 1963, his life was full of promise. In an instant, the experienced pilot transitioned from a free man to a prisoner held on spy charges by mainland China. Promised early on he would be returned to Taiwan, the weeks and months passed without change. Denounced by the government of Taiwan, Yeh became a man without a country. The son of a retired nationalist army general and educated in private schools, Yeh was forced to do the most menial jobs while in captivity: cleaning after farm animals, pulling weeds by hand, overhauling trucks and tallying workers' farm productions. Interrogations continued with the hope Yeh would break; the guards and interrogators were surprised at his unwavering position. Day after day, the examiners continued the questions about his flight, his aircraft, his squadron and even his family. They could not understand why he would not know all the intricacies of his aircraft and flight. After all, his was a new and special aircraft. Global changes between East and West provided slightly improved living conditions for prisoners. When the Chinese learned by accident that Yeh spoke English, they hatched a plan to use his language ability to their benefit while offering a better job using his skills. When Yeh's usefulness was exhausted, the Chinese offered him a chance to leave, but not without strings. After almost 20 years captive in China, the Taiwanese refused to allow him to return. Where could he go? Who could he turn to for help? Did his family know he was alive? Arranging his exit from China was another hurdle to clear. Using his ROCAF contacts from years past, 'Robin' found assistance where he did not expect it.

Linda Rios Bromley retired from Federal Civil Service after 33 years' employment in such locations as; Laughlin AFB in Texas, Charleston Naval Base in South Carolina, USAF Headquarters in Europe, Wiesbaden in Germany, NASA and Internal Revenue Service in Houston, Texas. She co-authored with Brig. Gen. Gerald E. McIlmoyle (Ret), *Remembering the Dragon Lady, Memoirs of the Men Who Experienced the Legend of the U-2 Spy Plane*. As a result of that book, she was invited to write a similar book for another USAF organization. Together with Jim Bard and Frank Hayes, Linda co-authored *We Served With Honor, Memories of the Men Who Served the 91st Strategic Reconnaissance Wing*. She has served as a member of the Board of Directors, Laughlin Heritage Foundation Museum in Del Rio, Texas. Linda is currently a member of Cypress Ink Blots Writers' Group in Cypress, Texas, and is the historian for the 91st SRW Association.

FLIGHT OF THE DRAGON

A TAIWANESE U-2 PILOT'S LONG JOURNEY TO FREEDOM

Linda Rios Bromley

Helion & Company

Helion & Company Limited
26 Willow Road
Solihull
West Midlands
B91 1UE
England
Tel. 0121 705 3393
Fax 0121 711 4075
Email: info@helion.co.uk
Website: www.helion.co.uk
Twitter: @helionbooks
Visit our blog http://blog.helion.co.uk/

Published by Helion & Company 2017
Designed and typeset by Farr out Publications, Wokingham, Berkshire
Cover designed by Paul Hewitt, Battlefield Design (www.battlefield-design.co.uk)
Printed by Lightning Source Limited, Milton Keynes, Buckinghamshire

Front cover: U-2 at sunrise. (Maureen Stephan)
Rear cover: ROCAF Black Cat U-2 squadron patch and U-2 full pressure suit demonstrated by Major Yang. (Author's own collection)

ISBN 978-1-911096-48-1

British Library Cataloguing-in-Publication Data.
A catalogue record for this book is available from the British Library.

For details of other military history titles published by Helion & Company Limited, contact the above address, or visit our website: http://www.helion.co.uk

We always welcome receiving book proposals from prospective authors.

For I know the plans I have for you, plans to prosper you and not to harm you, plans to give you hope and a future.

Jeremiah 29:11

Contents

List of Illustrations

Author's Notes

The Lockheed U-2 is still flown each day somewhere in the world. For example, NASA uses a fleet of specialized U-2s for high altitude research. In 2005, a U-2 captured photographs of the devastation in Louisiana and the US Gulf Coast by Hurricane Katrina. It has been used in countless crises and peacetime operations, making it one of the oldest airplanes in use today. The only active squadron of U-2 aircraft is stationed at Beale AFB, California.

Foreword

World history is filled with conflict between the powerful and those threatened. The Armed Truce between the Republic of China (ROC) and the Peoples Republic of China (PRC) is illustrative of that. It began with Chiang Kai-Shek, essentially the dictator of Mainland China and an ally of the US, who supported him with money and arms. At the same time, Mao Tse-tung, leader of his Communist followers in the mountains and deserts of Western China, was supported by the Soviet Union. After the Second World War it became clear from media reports that Chairman Mao was going to push Chiang Kai Shek and his Nationalists off the mainland and onto Taiwan and smaller islands in-between. By the time Dwight Eisenhower was elected President of the US, it was clear that he would never involve America in a land war in Asia. He had been through a logistics nightmare in Europe in the Second World War with the assembly of men and materials in the UK and Russia to conquer Nazi Germany and its allies. Subsequently President Eisenhower negotiated the demarcation of the North and South Vietnam into two independent countries.

In the 1960 campaign for president, Senator John Kennedy challenged Vice President Richard Nixon on his opinion of taking the US into war defending the PRC. The islands of Quemoy and Matsu, located between Formosa (Taiwan) and China, were shelled by the PRC. Communist China stated their objective was not the islands but to take over Formosa. President Eisenhower had authorized the CIA U-2 to penetrate the Soviet Iron Curtain. Consequently the use of the U-2 to penetrate the Bamboo Curtain of China was a natural consideration. With the shoot down of CIA pilot Francis G. Powers on May 1, 1960, U-2 overflights of denied territory ceased.

The training of Republic of China Air Force (ROCAF) pilots to fly the U-2 first began at Laughlin AFB, in south Texas. It was a time when the need for the U-2 had escalated to a high level worldwide and U-2 instructor pilots were in short supply. The pilots from the ROC were accomplished aviators and most were fluent in English. The only problem was the vernacular form of English; instructors had to be especially careful that their directions were fully understood. Instructors knew that the Soviets would supply Communist China with their SA-2 Guideline missile which had demonstrated its prowess in the shoot down of Powers in 1960 and Major Rudolph Anderson, USAF, in 1962 over Cuba. USAF instructor pilots in the 4080th Strategic Reconnaissance Wing would be essentially placing the ROC pilots into the Chinese Dragon's mouth. It behooved the instructors to ensure the ROC pilots knew the U-2 inside and out. They also had to learn the best ways to defeat the Soviet SA-2 missile once it had been launched. The Guideline missile was out of energy by the time it approached the flight altitude of the U-2, and it could not turn with the U-2. Instructors trained ROC pilots in our evasion technique which was to do an 'S' turn. It entailed a 90 degree turn into the missile, then an immediate 180 degree turn back, then another immediate 180 degree turn back and a 90 degree to return on course. That maneuver proved infallible. However, the key was seeing the Guideline missile as it rose in its intercept curve. As they were sent off to do battle for their country, everyone who had helped train the ROC pilots and maintenance crews were honored to have known them and had great respect for their ability and courage. As with all Allied fighting men, their Comrades in Arms wished them well and prayed for their safety.

Gerald E. McIlmoyle, Brig. Gen. USAF (Ret.) U-2 pilot 1959 to 1964

Preface

Soaring near the edge of the stratosphere, the sleek, silver jet neared the island the pilot called home. Alone in the cockpit with only the whine of the engine, he could see the curvature of the earth with the dark blue sky beyond. It was an awesome experience to witness such a spectacle and to realize that he was one of few humans who had ever flown so high. Indeed, he had been specially selected for the job. He was grateful for the confidence in his ability that brought him to this point. As he sat almost motionless in the tiny cockpit, his pressure suit and helmet gave him a sense of being trapped in a capsule hurtling through space.

After the eight-hour reconnaissance flight, he was exhausted; but he had to remain alert. His was a job that required constant attention to several details simultaneously. There was so much that could go wrong in an instant. Prior to his flight, he had been briefed about the weather in the target area, the photographs he was expected to capture and the possibility of a hostile threat. He monitored the instruments in front of him; the altimeter displayed the correct altitude for this part of his flight, the airspeed was steady and the hum of the engine throttled back to 92 percent power at 74,000 feet. The last thing he expected was what everyone in the brotherhood of pilots understood was a sound they never want to hear: silence, the signal of an engine flameout.

Home, the island off the nose of his aircraft, was now clearly visible. Within a short time he would be having dinner with his young bride.

As he scanned the horizon, the fiery projectile streaking toward him brought him back to the moment. His training had prepared him for response to the emergency; his expertise immediately kicked in. Evasive action was instantaneous, but not soon enough. A bright red-orange glow filled his windscreen; the concussion jerked him without mercy.

Impact.
Free fall.
Contact.

Acknowledgments

In 2004 my husband, Bill, introduced me to Robin Yeh. We had an instant connection when I learned he trained at Laughlin Air Force Base in Del Rio, Texas, where I grew up and attended school. After a short time, I knew I wanted to write about his experience and Robin allowed me to interview him numerous times. I published my first book, titled *Freedom Flight*, which chronicled some details of Robin's confinement in Communist China. In 2005 I was invited to a reunion of the 4080th Strategic Reconnaissance Wing veterans and their families. At that time I met the Black Cat pilots who were honored guests. All were gracious, charming, and willing to answer my many questions. Following the publication of *Freedom Flight*, I wanted to write a re-make of the book to provide more details to this fascinating story. Duncan Rogers and Helion & Company Ltd. allowed me to do that. After unforeseen delays, the story that follows, now titled *Flight of the Dragon*, is a more thorough account of Robin Yeh's experience.

There are many people who have helped with the content of this book. I wish to recognize them for their patience in answering many questions.

Robert Birkett – USAF (Retired) U-2 pilot provided his expertise of the aircraft and the Taiwan/US relations.

Neal E. Coltrane – USAF (Retired), provided historical documentation on the U-2 program.

General Mike Hua – (Retired), a ROCAF U-2 pilot, gave his permission for me to use some details from his book, *Lost Black Cats, Story of Two Captured Chinese U-2 Pilots*.

Chris I – a ROCAF U-2 pilot, shared his expertise through responses to my questions via many emails.

Xu Lin – shared many photos from his personal collection. He spent countless hours at the National Archives in Washington, DC reviewing photos taken by ROCAF U-2 pilots.

John Raines – retired CIA specialist, knew all the ROCAF U-2 pilots while he was assigned to Taoyuan Air Base. I had many lengthy phone conversations with John. Anyone who has met John understands those were very long phone calls.

Mory Tsai – retired ROCAF U-2 pilot, provided detailed information about the squadron and some of its functions.

Robert (Gimo) Yang – was the second commander of the Black Cat Squadron. I spent time with him at his home in Las Vegas as he recalled many events of the Black Cats.

Steve Yip – Robin's younger brother, provided me with detailed information about the family living arrangements at their home in Canton. Steve's daughter, Anita, received my emails and replied to me with his answers.

Ink Blots Writers' Group – Stan, Gordon, Heather, Julie and Linda: thanks for your valuable critiques.

Thanks especially to Duncan Rogers and his staff at Helion & Company for their patience with the many delays incurred with this manuscript.

1

Early Life

World events in 1934 ran the gamut of slow simmering revolutions to human interest stories. Some of the headlines were: "USSR joined the League of Nations"; "Bruno Hauptman arrested for kidnapping Charles Lindberg's son"; "Adolph Hitler expanded German Army and Navy"; "Winston Churchill expressed to British Prime Minister Stanley Baldwin, Do not underestimate German air power"; "New York Giants defeated the Chicago Bears 30-13 for the National Football League Championship".

On the other side of the world, a celebration in the Yeh household in Canton, Guandong Province, China, announced the birth of Chang-di Yeh on November 1, 1934. The third child of father, Wei-Shen Yeh, and mother, Shi-Wueng Shu, Chang-di experienced an almost idyllic childhood. He spent his early life in Canton, population: 236,694. His siblings were one older brother and sister with four younger brothers and a sister. Chang-di's father had been a major general in the Nationalist Army under General Chiang Kai Shek. After retirement, his father worked as director of a bank in Canton and later in Shanghai.

Guandong was well known for its exquisite porcelain. The formula for the porcelain was a well-kept secret. Trade ships reached the port of Canton via Macau and Hong Kong up the Pearl River to their destination. Early Americans prized Canton porcelain which was the only durable one available until the mid-1800s. Common table ware, referred to as everyday china, for Americans from Knox, Hancock, Paul Revere, Quincy and a score of other well-known citizens, who ate their meals from old blue Canton porcelain. The entire process, including: to order, design, paint, and deliver to America was approximately a two year period.

The Yeh family enjoyed a comfortable upper-middle class lifestyle in Canton. They actually lived in a six-story building that had been converted from a commercial property at 278 Da Xin Lu (literally translated: Big New Road). The street was a well-known location where many artists created the finest ivory carvings, valued throughout the world. Other parts of the city were known for China's traditional paintings using a brush dipped in black or colored ink. Scrolls, lacquerware and folding screens with the artwork decorated many homes, including the Yeh's.

The family home was constructed with a center corridor from the days when the building served several businesses. With little modifications, the shop spaces became living areas for the family. The first floor served as the garage for their family car, a black Chevy four-door sedan. Typical of housing in the 1940's, there was no heating system when temperatures plummeted to 25 degrees Fahrenheit. Everyone snuggled in under mounds of blankets and quilts and wore several layers of clothing. The kitchen was the warmest room in the house when meals were being prepared for the family.

The parents' rooms were on the second floor, and the Yeh sisters occupied the third floor. Due to the large space available on the third floor, the family also dined there with food delivered via a dumbwaiter from the kitchen on the fifth floor. The boys' dormitory occupied the fourth floor; the sixth floor roof became their playground and kite flying area.

The Yeh brothers often engaged in kite fighting, a challenging game to cut one another's strings made of glass. The bigger kites were an especially good target, and whoever flew one was an easy target. The brothers thought it great fun when a challenger's kite was cut and released to float away.

A bomb shelter, with an earthen floor, had been constructed under their home in the event of a Japanese air raid. The boys often played there throwing mud balls at each other until one of the brothers went crying to their mother when the balls were too big or thrown too hard. Often their mother stopped the game altogether, and then the brothers pursued other activities to entertain themselves.

As a boy, Chang-di was fascinated with the airplanes that occasionally flew overhead. His daydreams were filled with the grace, beauty and mystery of flight. Airplanes were his favorite toys. He imagined himself flying over foreign lands. Though his understanding of a world outside China was limited, Chang-di spent hours studying his aircraft. Even on harsh winter days he spent hours outdoors 'flying' his airplanes.

Chang-di's mother managed the household with assistance of part-time help and raised her large family with love and affection. She was a devout Buddhist, but other members of the family were less attached to any religion. While in some parts of China, home remedies and herbal medicines were popular where doctors were not available, Shi-Wueng Shu assumed responsibility for the health needs and well-being of the family. When a member of her family fell ill, a qualified medical specialist provided treatment and medicines. With six active boys, at least one was seeing the doctor for minor injuries when a game became too rough.

During the years prior to 1949, the six boys and two girls of the Yeh family grew up comfortable and secure. Chang-di's brothers were Chang Yun (Warren), Chang Chao (Creek), Chang Li (Steve), Chang-Hsi (Richard) and Chang Ti (Joseph). His sisters were Chang Ling (Selina) and Chang Wo (Doris). The brothers and sisters enjoyed the companionship of their two dogs and two cats. A pond stocked with koi provided tranquility for the family, especially for the adults after a busy day.

The Yeh sons and daughters attended a private school for which their father paid tuition. There were no free schools. Their parents believed that teachers at the church school were better qualified than at other facilities. They studied world history, math, science and English as a foreign language. Chang-di's mother considered it her responsibility to monitor her children's education to ensure they all earned good grades. She also made sure the children's clothes were in good condition for school, both clean and repaired. It was not unusual when the boys came in from play with torn pants or shirts.

Each school day, the children were awakened by their mother. After a quick wash up, they dressed in the clothes she laid out for them. Breakfast of porridge or noodles awaited them before their chauffer took them to school. When Chang-di and his sister Doris were at boarding school, their meals were provided there.

Chang-di attended elementary school in Hong Kong, middle school in Canton and high school in Shanghai where he and Doris lived with their father who directed the operations of the bank. Chang-di's formal education consisted of 12 grades. Throughout his education, he excelled at math, his favorite subject. He participated on the school soccer team; his size and speed made him a quick and agile player. At the beginning of each school year, he looked forward to a greater challenge, whether in academics or on the sports field.

Chang-di learned about American government in his civics class. But American movies

The Yeh Family. Top: Father Wei-Sheng holding son Chang-Ti. Middle Row: Chang-Yun (Warren), Chang-Hsi (Richard) at his father's left side, Mother Shi-Weung Shu, Chang-Li (Steve) near his mother. Front row: Chang-Ling (Serena), Chang-Wo (Doris), paternal grandmother, Chang-Hsao (Creek) beside grandmother, Chang-di (Robin) aged 8. (Robin Yeh's collection)

sparked his curiosity about the West. The first American movie he saw was in 1942 when he was about eight years old, *Robin Hood* starring Errol Flynn, which left a lasting impression. Although the movie was in English with no translation to Mandarin, the action captured his interest and conveyed the story. The movie was even in color! He saw other films that depicted a Western lifestyle of luxurious cars, large houses and fancy clothes. However, the movies featuring airplanes riveted his interest. Airplanes of various sizes and speed consumed his attention and imagination.

Chang-di's curiosity was a trait he retained from an early age. One of Chang-di's fondest memories in Canton was a day when he talked the chauffeur into letting him drive the family car. Although only age 14, he had observed the chauffeur each time he was in the car. The chauffeur dutifully reported to Chang-di's dad about the newest driver; but, fortunately Wei-Sheng was not angry. Instead, he gave permission for continued driving lessons. At the time no license or permit was required to operate a vehicle. However, an early incident, when he was alone behind the wheel, had a lifelong memory. He had been driving only a few months when young Chang-di's vehicle approached a rickshaw, but he applied the brake too slowly. The car bumped the rickshaw which forced the driver to run ahead in 'high gear'. Chang-di stopped his car and ran to catch the driver and cart. The shaken rickshaw driver assured Chang-di neither he nor the cart were injured or damaged. That day a very grateful Chang-di drove his car directly home. The lesson he learned was to be alert and prepared for any situation, one that would serve him well in the future.

The Yeh family celebrated the Autumn Moon festival on August 15 each year, a centuries-old holiday which marked the end of the harvest season. Although the Yehs were not farmers, it was a holiday celebrated by everyone as an opportunity to gather with friends and family. The young Yehs looked forward to attending the festival; it was a special time with delicious food, lively music and entertainment.

Chinese New Year, the most important of the traditional festivities, marked the end of the winter season. The holiday has its origins in many centuries past, but is celebrated each year with customs and traditions passed on by generations of each family. Children especially looked forward to the New Year celebration in expectation of presents from friends and family. The Yeh house was thoroughly cleaned to sweep away any ill fortune and make way for incoming good luck. Red colored paper cutouts with themes of good fortune, happiness, wealth and longevity decorated the home. New Year's Eve, celebrated with a huge dinner, included many foods specially prepared for the holiday. Fireworks in their large back yard after the dinner provided entertainment for everyone. The brothers especially enjoyed the fun of the fireworks, the noise and color overhead. The following morning the children greeted their parents to wish them a healthy and Happy New Year. In turn each received presents or money in red envelopes. Chinese New Year in 1949 was the last they would celebrate as a family in Canton.

As early as the 16th century, Taiwan was colonized by groups of explorers: the Austronesians, Dutch, Han Chinese from Fujian and Guangdong of mainland China, and even the Spanish. Since that time, the island was called Formosa, derived from the Portuguese meaning 'Beautiful Island', and subsequently by its Chinese name, Taiwan. The ruling Chinese political party from 1927 to 1949, Kuomintang (KMT), was founded on August 25, 1912 by Sun Yat-sen. The name translates as 'China's National People's Party' and was commonly known as the Chinese Nationalists. After Sun's death, the party was dominated by Chiang Kai-shek. Though the Nationalists lost the civil war with the Communist Party of China in 1949, it became a major political movement of the Republic of China based in Taiwan. Japan renounced all territorial rights to Taiwan in 1952 in the San Francisco Peace Treaty. The KMT ruled Taiwan as a single-party state for 40 years, until democratic reforms were implemented by Chiang Kai-shek's son, Chiang Ching-kuo in the 1980s.

In October 1949 the lives of the Yeh family changed dramatically when Mao Tse-tung seized power in China. Middle class citizens, like the Yehs, were at great risk of being imprisoned or killed because their democratic beliefs were in conflict with Mao's communist doctrine. Wei-Sheng feared for his life and fled from Shanghai to the British Crown Colony of Hong Kong with Chang-di and Doris who were attending school. The remainder of the family followed in the chauffeur-driven car from Canton. Unable to take treasured family mementos and possessions, they carried only heavy-laden suitcases with their money and gold bars to start their new lives.

Shi-Weung Shu joined her husband and regrouped her sons and daughters at their home in Hong Kong. Six months later, they flew together to the Republic of China. They could have continued to live in Hong Kong, but Wei-Sheng had been a strong supporter of General Chiang Kai-Shek since his own service as an Army officer. It was a personal decision he made to continue his support of the popular general.

Shanghai was the center of much of Mao's Red Guards' and revolutionaries' terrorism and destruction before it spread throughout the country. At Mao's direction, marauding bands of teenagers wearing red armbands, roamed the streets of Shanghai, targeting upper middle class neighborhoods. The lawless Red Guards stormed private homes, hauling off books, artwork, antique paintings and furniture to be destroyed, sometimes burned in the street. The owners stood helpless as their priceless treasures were destroyed on the spot, while the Red Guards quoted Mao. Other times the valuables would be presented to the state as evidence against the resident. Condemned by the Red Guards, residents were required to attend 'struggle' meetings where they were expected to confess to their offenses against the state, whether real or trumped up charges. Some residents maintained innocence but were still sent to prison not knowing the charges against them, other than they had offended the state. Indefinite prison terms awaited many because of their associations with foreigners.

When he neared the end of high school, Chang-di's interest in airplanes had become more than mere childhood fascination. He was interested in pursuing a flight career. When his older brother, Warren, entered the Republic of China Air Force (ROCAF), Chang-di was impressed with his brother's new career and striking uniform. Not only did his brother wear a sharp-looking uniform and fly sleek aircraft, but also, young Chang-di observed almost wistfully, pilots attracted the attention of beautiful young women.

Chang-di questioned his brother at every opportunity about military aircraft. He studied books and pictures and memorized the characteristics of the P-51, P-38 and P-47 aircraft. He was able to identify them as they flew overhead. Now in his dreams he visualized himself in the cockpit. Following in Warren's footsteps, Chang-di was determined to become a cadet and fly military airplanes. Warren was aware that his younger brother had the 'right stuff' to become a ROCAF officer. As an instructor at the ROCAF Academy, Warren had the inside track on enrollments and openings in future classes. Chang-di learned from Warren that there was a chance he could be selected to attend the Academy. Early in 1950 Warren advised him to report for a physical examination, a preliminary of the selection process. A short time later, Warren announced to an excited Chang-di he had been accepted to the Academy for training. Later, their younger brother, Chang-ti (Joseph), entered the ROCAF Academy in 1959 following the career paths of his father and two older brothers. However, Joseph's career was cut short due to health issues that prevented him from achieving his dream.

The Republic of China Air Force Academy (ROCAFA) was initially established in 1928 in Nanjing. It was then called the Central Army Academy's Aviation Corps. After relocations and renaming the organization, in 1938 the official title became Air Force Academy located at Gangshan, Kaohsiung, Taiwan. Chang-di entered the ROCAF Academy in 1950 and studied diligently to reach the first of his many goals. He was not assigned to any academic classes that Warren instructed to eliminate any hint of conflict of interest. However, Warren felt his own reputation was at stake for recommending his brother for admission. He was eager to confirm his confidence in Chang-di's skills. To bolster his opinion, he scheduled a check flight with Chang-di in a North American AT6 Texan advanced trainer. Following the flight, Warren's pride in his younger brother's ability and professionalism confirmed his support was well founded. Chang-di graduated in 1952 as a commissioned Warrant Officer. It was only the beginning of his advancement in the Air Force, and his commitment to his new career.

Following his graduation, Chang-di and 12 of his Academy classmates reported to the 11th Fighting Group at Hsin-chu Air Base. As a member of the group, he flew the P-47, T-33 and F-86, and in 1956 he was promoted to captain. Colonel Shichu (Gimo)

Robin suited up for a flight standing with General Chiang Kai-Shek in front of a RF-101 aircraft. (Robin Yeh's collection)

Yang, Commander of the 6th Reconnaissance Group (RG), 12th Squadron, had learned of Chang-di's flying proficiency, and offered him an opportunity to join the 6th RG. It was a great honor to be recognized for his aviation skills and to be part of the select few recruited for the 6th Recon Group. Chang-di eagerly accepted Colonel Yang's offer.

Fighter pilots have long had a reputation as hard-working, fun-loving men who daily risked their lives in supersonic aircraft. Chang-di acknowledged the risks of his career, and he thrived on it. Each day he was in an airplane, he felt a fulfillment that was only truly understood by others in the brotherhood of pilots. He was honored to have such an experience, and his skill and ability earned him a place among the best.

As a member of the 4th Squadron, 6th Recon Group, he flew the Republic RF-84F Thunderflash, an American-built swept-wing photo reconnaissance aircraft. Flying in the single cockpit, he was totally responsible for all aspects of the aircraft and the photographic missions he was assigned. Chang-di later flew the McDonnell RF-101F Voodoo, a twin-engine, supersonic reconnaissance aircraft. He was the first to fly a photo mission with the RF-101 over Mainland China in June 1961, and returned with clear photos of five newly constructed air bases along the coast. The photo intelligence from the flight was reported directly to the Supreme Commander of the ROCAF, Generalissimo Chiang Kai-shek. General Chiang paid a special visit to Taoyuan Air Base to recognize Chang-di's achievement, and was photographed with him in front of the RF-101. Following a year in training for the RF-101F in Okinawa, he returned to Taiwan and subsequently received a promotion to major.

His flight leader at the 11th Fighter Wing, Major Wen, was a classmate of Chang-di's brother, Warren. When the base sponsored an event to invite families and friends to view the aircraft on the flight line, Wen invited his girlfriend, Hsio (Helen) Tung, and she brought her younger sister, Betty. Chang-di met Betty and gave her a tour of the event. He showed her the equipment pilots wore for a flight. She sat in the cockpit of an F-86 while Chang-di explained many of the features in the cramped space.

Chang-di was captivated with the charming young woman. He was 23; she was 16 and still attending high school. They began a casual relationship, meeting when they each found the time. To give a semblance of chaperoned outings, Helen would accompany them, but she conveniently disappeared after a short time. Chang-di and Betty had an opportunity to get better acquainted when they went out for ice cream or sodas. Occasionally, they went to an early movie. Because she was still in school, Betty's father imposed a curfew of 9:00 p.m. Their relationship blossomed, and they spent as much time together as their schedules allowed.

After Betty completed her high school studies, she worked as a teller at a local bank for three years. Because of her interest in Chang-di, she applied for and was hired for a sales position at the Taoyuan Base Exchange. Betty enjoyed her new job and especially being at the ROCAF base where there was an occasional opportunity to see Chang-di if for only a brief moment. The US established the Office of Military Assistance Advisory Group (MAAG) in Taiwan to provide support to the South Vietnamese government. When a secretarial position was announced, Betty applied and was selected for the job.

2

Whispers of the Dragon Lady

Following the descent of the 'Bamboo Curtain' when the Communists seized control of the country in 1949, the outside world learned little about what transpired inside China. US satellites took high altitude photographs, but the poor quality and clarity rendered the process mostly useless. US President Dwight Eisenhower's request for more accurate intelligence information on the Soviet Union was the incentive for a new aircraft design. Modified bombers overflew the Soviet Union, but the aircraft were vulnerable to anti-aircraft fire and a number of border flights were shot down.

Awarded the contract, Skunk Works, a division of the Lockheed Aircraft Corporation developed a high altitude aircraft that would be hard to detect and impossible to shoot down. The CL-282 AQUATONE was designated as the development name. The official title took a bit more consideration. The new plane could not be identified with a 'B' for bomber nor an 'F' for fighter as its purpose did not fit either of those categories. The USAF decided to call it a utility plane. The final designation for the new aircraft was the U-2.

When Lockheed received approval for their design on December 9, 1954, the company's Skunk Works, headed by Clarence "Kelly" Johnson, began a gruelling pace to meet the deadline. Under a heavy veil of secrecy, Kelly and only 81 people, including 25 engineers, began work on the design. The project was so secret that the government's first check was made out to Kelly personally and mailed to his home address.

A pivotal feature of the aircraft was the camera system which was like no other ever designed. Jim Baker, an optical engineer from the Massachusetts Institute of Technology (MIT) and Edwin Land, developer of the Polaroid camera, were tasked to design the camera system for this unique aircraft. The specifications seemed impossible to meet: capable of photographing ground areas from altitudes in excess of 70,000 feet, weigh less than 500 pounds and compact enough to fit inside the equipment bay. Baker and Land worked with the Hycon Company of Monrovia, California to develop the camera known as the Hycon 73B, later known by technicians simply as the 'B' configuration.

Pratt and Whitney produced an engine that would perform at an altitude of 70,000 feet and higher. The cockpit was partially pressurized to enable pilots to fly for up to 10 hours without full pressure suits. Pilots were custom fitted with partial pressure suits by the D. G. Clark Company of Worcester, Massachusetts. One of the most radical parts of the aircraft's design was the bicycle gear system. The reason for the bicycle landing gear concept was simple: weight reduction. An estimated 2,000 feet of altitude was gained over use of the more conventional landing gear. Flying the U-2 aircraft was not for the faint of heart; in fact, it was considered one of the most challenging aircraft in the inventory to fly and required a high degree of skill and ability from its pilots. The difficulty experienced by seasoned pilots who flew the U-2 nicknamed it the 'Dragon Lady' meaning the aircraft was extremely unforgiving.

In the spring of 1958, the US established a Central Intelligence Agency (CIA) detachment in Taiwan headed by Dr. Ray Cline. Very early in his new assignment, he formed a working relationship with Chiang Ching Kuo, Deputy Security General of the ROC National Security Council and son of President Chiang Kai Shek. The two intelligence leaders formed a bond that supported a mutual cooperation. To lend support to the ROCAF operation, the US supplied state of the art electronic signal recorders and communications receivers.

On a visit to the US following the May 1960 shoot down of a U-2 inside the Soviet Union, Chiang Ching Kuo discussed the break between the People's Republic of China (PRC) and the Soviet Union. He suggested the time was right to collect intelligence on nuclear and scientific technology targets. Many in Taiwan believed that the PRC's anti-aircraft weapons were too primitive to deal with the high-flying U-2 aircraft. The CIA and US National Security Council wholeheartedly concurred, and President Eisenhower approved the plan on behalf of the US.

In 1956 the ROCAF Technical Research Unit was assigned to the Department of Air Force Intelligence, directly under the supervision of Colonel I. Based at Hsin-chu, the unit became known as the 34th Squadron. It had an expanded mission including Electronic Countermeasures (ECM) to detect radar installations of the Communist air defense. With the completion of the facilities, the efficiency of the group improved dramatically. The technical unit identified intelligence gathered from monitored messages of the PRC air defense actions against the U-2 flights over the mainland. The group relayed information to the U-2 pilot through coded messages so he could take evasive action to avoid missile attack. By monitoring the PRC radar stations, Taoyuan Control Center knew the position of a U-2 during flights over the mainland.

In the 1950s, the ROCAF frequently conducted their own photo reconnaissance overflights of the PRC with RB-57A/D aircraft provided by the US. Photographic film analysis was mostly performed by the US CIA field agents stationed at the Taoyuan Air Base. In the early 1950s, monitoring the PRC activity on the opposite side of the China Strait fell to a small, unsophisticated photo lab of the 12th Photographic Reconnaissance Squadron (PRS) at Taoyuan AFB. Colonel Yung Pang Tsai headed the photo intelligence unit, film processing and interpretation of overflight missions. The darkrooms of the photo laboratory were housed in an old Japanese barracks. Film processing facilities were located in a former US Army Air Corps facility. When a power failure occurred at the most inopportune times, technicians simply moved the wet, still-developing aerial film outside to dry.

Chiang Ching Kuo briefed his president and top level officers regarding the agreement reached in Washington, DC. The presentation included high resolution photos taken by a U-2 over the capital of Tibet and the western region of China. When they viewed the clarity of the film, they approved the project and preparations began almost immediately. Taoyuan AFB was selected to be the home of the ROCAF U-2 operation and the joint operations became one of the most successful examples of cooperation between the US and Taiwan.

Colonel I Fu-En (pronounced E Foo In), served as Chief, ROCAF Intelligence from 1955-1965, and directed highly classified missions that were critical to both Taiwan and the US. In 1955 Colonel I learned the CIA was interested in working with the ROCAF on gathering radar intelligence, with primary interest being mainland Communist China. Technical representatives (tech reps) of US government contractors came to Taoyuan to support the U-2 arrival and set up shop with their equipment for the joint operation, known as Project Razor. The unit of US officials and tech reps became known as Detachment H; ROCAF designated their unit as the 35th Squadron.

Colonel I Fu En and Dr. T. W. Yu, Minister of National Defense, presided over the ceremony on October 18, 1960 to open the new film processing and photo intelligence facility, nicknamed the Night Owl Squadron. The name referred to the time most of the work would be performed, late at night following the arrival of an incoming recon flight. A number of US officers and officials were present to reinforce commitment to Taiwan.

The Lockheed P-38 Lightning flew reconnaissance missions in the early summer of 1951 and confirmed the presence of MiG-15 fighters at Shanghai. Later that year, a North American B-25 Mitchell on a night recon mission identified numerous Soviet Il-28 bombers in Qunqiao AFB, Zhejiang Province of the PRC. Colonel Tsai reported the find to ROCAF leaders who immediately alerted the US Far East Air Force.

In 1954 Colonel Tsai and a select group of ROCAF officials were invited to observe Navy photo interpreters onboard the aircraft carrier USS *Boxer* in the Pacific Ocean between the Philippines and Taiwan. The Navy showed an oblique photo which they suspected to be anti-aircraft gun positions or specialized military equipment. The ROCAF officers identified the construction as that of traditional Chinese family residences for multiple generations living together, similar to other structures located in the southeast provinces of China. The meeting confirmed for the ROCAF officials that the US had photo interpretation capabilities which far exceeded their own.

By 1954, ROCAF photo intelligence identified new airfields under construction at Luqiano and Daishan, in Zhejiang Province. By April 1955 technicians discovered four additional airfields under construction with a familiar Soviet-designed pattern. They identified a 1.5 million gallon fuel depot for a railroad being built between Yingtan, in Jiangxi Province to Amoy, in Fujian Province. With this information, the US provided the ROCAF with a squadron of Lockheed RT-33 Shooting Star aircraft. The two-seater trainer was reconfigured for the elimination of one seat to accommodate installation of specialized camera equipment. At this time ROCAF photo intelligence operations consolidated the 12th PRS, the new 4th PRS, and the Photo Tech Squadron into the 6th Photo Recon Group (PRG). With RT-33s flying almost night and day missions across the Strait of China, the PRG was not lacking for work. By the end of 1956 photo intelligence had confirmed construction of four more airfields in Fujian and Canton provinces. ROCAF and US officials were alerted to the serious buildups in progress.

Considering the expansion of PRC military complexes, the US delivered RF-86s to assist the RT-33s. By the end of 1956 the primary ROCAF photo reconnaissance aircraft was the Republic Aircraft Company RF-84F Thunderflash. The increased reconnaissance flights meant expanded photo processing and interpretation. The photo recon unit then worked around the clock. Dr. T. W. Yu became a primary supporter of the overflight photo intelligence. He made frequent visits to Taoyuan to review recent aerial photo coverage, and questioned the status and changes of the military targets, making recommendations accordingly.

The first U-2 arrived at Taoyuan in early December 1960, disassembled in crates onboard a USAF C-133. In 1961 the 35th Squadron, nicknamed Black Cat Squadron, was formed with Colonel Lu (Michael) Xiliang as its first commander, and Colonel Shichu (Gimo) Yang followed as the next leader. Secrecy was paramount, and the squadron operated under the cover of a high altitude weather research unit located on an isolated part of the base. Assigned to the unit were 26 ROCAF pilots; seven in the first group completed U-2 training in the US as others awaited orders for training. The unit frequently had only two or three spy planes in its inventory due to maintenance issues and occasionally the number was down to one. During the life of the squadron, nineteen U-2s were delivered to the Black Cat Squadron. The squadron flew 220 operational missions, including 102 surveillance flights over the PRC.

Shortly after the 1962 New Year's holidays, Project Razor received authorization from the highest offices of the ROC and the US for the first U-2 overflight mission designated as flight GRC-100. Major Hwei Chen, an experienced photo recon pilot since 1953, was assigned the premier flight. In 1957 flying a RF-84F Chen successfully photographed a PRC MiG-17 in flight with the forward oblique camera. At 7:00 a.m. on January 13, 1962, Chen departed Taoyuan AFB. He climbed to 40,000 feet and headed northwest along the coast south of Wenchou. Chen covered all the planned targets and returned to Taoyuan at 3:40 p.m., almost nine hours after takeoff. When Chen arrived, the 35th Squadron personnel on duty were jubilant. Chen's aircraft had barely reached the ramp when the CIA reps immediately took custody of the film and shipped it under the strictest security to the 67th Recon Tech Squadron at USAF Yakota AFB, Japan. ROCAF photo interpreters and technicians were disappointed they were not involved, but they awaited the shipment of 20 rolls of duplicates of mission GRC-100. Six very excited ROCAF photo interpreters rolled the duplicate film onto their light tables and performed as they were trained. They were shocked to see the clarity of the film and detail captured of the target areas. Sites were identified at Shiang Cheng Tzi, information the US had been eager to learn about.

With this capability, ROCAF was now able to cover military installations, bomb production facilities, fuel depots, and other significant target areas. Beginning in 1962, overflight coverage was expanded to all of mainland China; nothing was out of reach of the Black Cats' U-2 flights. In February Flight GRC-102 was completed, and curiously, film arrived from the US instead of Japan as had been expected. Targets were identified in the northeast region of mainland China near the Soviet border. The sensitivity and security for handling U-2 overflight film required a special location. The Night Owl Squadron relocated to a bomb-proof bunker, nicknamed The Roman Temple, to operate with the highest security.

An embarrassing turn of events occurred in July when film was delivered to the Night Owl Squadron, and interpreters reported for duty. The film rolled onto the light table, but interpreters found an inconsistent mission number and the terrain of the mainland was not the same as they expected. Packed in four shipping containers, a total of 24 rolls of film revealed the coverage of Cuba. Night Owl personnel reported the find to the US team. CIA specialists quickly retrieved the film and shipped it out to another interpretation destination. That mishap led the Night Owl team to conclude that all U-2 film was shipped to the US for processing and duplication.

In March 1961 mission film was loaded on a CIA C-47 for transport to Washington, DC. En route, the crew declared an inflight emergency when one of the engines failed. To eliminate as much weight as possible for the aircraft to remain airborne, the crew jettisoned 43 boxes of highly classified film over the mountainous region of Williamsport, Pennsylvania. The pilot declared an emergency landing at a nearby airport and notified the CIA. Teams of CIA personnel immediately notified local police to secure the area where the boxes went down. After considerable searching, all 43 boxes were recovered intact. As a result of these two events, the Night Owl Squadron was then authorized to process U-2 overflight mission film at Taoyuan. The squadron was offered equipment and supplies to begin precision processing in the new bunker facility. Hycon's tech rep and Kodak experts installed and tested the equipment within two weeks.

Early in 1963 Chang-di was offered a chance to attend U-2 flight training in the US. He knew little about the aircraft because it was so new and its operation top secret. However, he had heard rumors among squadron pilots about its capabilities, and he was indeed curious. He was grateful his performance evaluations and flying skills had been recognized. A small select group of pilots had been selected to attend the first U-2 training class in the US, and Major Yeh was extremely honored to be included among the chosen few.

Hsiuh "Mike" Hua recalled being selected in the first group of pilots in 1963. A clandestine phone call at his residence one evening directed him to report to Air Force Headquarters the following morning. There he joined 11 other pilots who flew to Okinawa that day for physical exams. Three months later he was en route to the US with five other pilots. The details of his TDY were so secret that he was completely unaware of his mission in the US or even how long he would be there. It was only when the USAF officers told his group they were there to learn to fly the U-2 for reconnaissance missions that Mike Hua fully understood the secrecy required. Their destination was Laughlin AFB, Del Rio, Texas.

Following another physical exam, the group dressed in the required pressure suits for a session in the high altitude chamber. Chang-di's RF-101 flights required the partial pressure suit making it unnecessary for him to try the suit in the high altitude chamber this time. Chang-di was scheduled with the first group of pilots to go to the US for six months' training. Unlike the selection process for USAF pilots, the ROCAF pilots' records had been screened in advance. The squadron commander notified each pilot he had been selected for reassignment to the Black Cat Squadron and training at a USAF base. As the classification of the U-2 operation became less sensitive and the prestige to be a U-2 pilot increased, an application process was established for prospective candidates.

Before reporting to the US, many of the ROCAF pilots chose American nicknames, such as Mike, Tiger, Spike and Tom. Chang-di selected the nickname "Robin" recalling his childhood movie hero, Robin Hood. Survival training was a course routinely planned early on for fighter pilots, and Robin was also scheduled to attend. Due to scheduling conflicts, he had not received a survival training date before he began flying the U-2. Suddenly his life was moving at a rapid pace. Robin was engaged to be married to his fiancée, Betty, and the wedding ceremony and reception had already been scheduled. The wedding date, he learned, conflicted with his reporting date for U-2 training. After a meeting with his squadron commander, Colonel Lu, he was permitted to attend U-2 training with the second group of trainees. Three months after the wedding, he said goodbye to his new bride and prepared for his life-changing adventure.

3

Up Close and Personal

In the spring of 1963, Robin traveled from Taiwan to Laughlin AFB in Texas with other pilots in his group. Only two bases conducted U-2 flight training: Laughlin and Davis Monthan AFB in Tucson, Arizona. Both were located in the southwest part of the US and offered excellent weather conditions for maximum flight time. It was in Texas that he began his training with the USAF 4080th Strategic Reconnaissance Wing (SRW).

The 4080th Strategic Reconnaissance Wing (Light) was organized May 1, 1956 at Turner AFB, Georgia and was assigned to the 40th Air Division of the Strategic Air Command. Operational squadrons assigned to the Wing were the 4025th, 4028th and 4029th Strategic Reconnaissance Squadrons (SRS). On April 1, 1957, the Wing was reassigned directly to Second Air Force and relocated to Laughlin AFB, Texas. The 4029th SRS and 4025th SRS were discontinued on January 1, 1960 and June 15, 1960, respectively. The Wing was re-designated as the 4080th Strategic Wing and relocated to Davis Monthan AFB, Arizona on July 1, 1963, and subsequently reassigned to the 12th Strategic Aerospace Division. The 4080th Strategic Reconnaissance Wing was discontinued on June 25, 1966, 10 years and one month after it was organized.

First group of U-2 trainees to Laughlin AFB. From left: Major Chan Hia, USAF Officer, Major Mike Hua, Major Shia, USAF Officer, Major Gen Wang, USAF Officer, Major Yang and Major Tiger Wang. (Author's own collection)

In addition to learning a new aircraft, Robin had many unique experiences, both cultural and professional, during that time. West Texas, flat and barren, was a stark contrast to the mountainous island of his home in Taiwan. Adjusting to the desert-like climate of south Texas, in summer was not really a problem; he focused on the reason he was there. It was exciting to be part of this history-making event, and Robin absorbed everything associated with the training experience. Robin was exactly where he wanted to be and felt immense satisfaction to have a job that he loved. He looked forward to the challenge of flying a new and significantly more complex aircraft that was the focus of attention within the intelligence community and part of top secret US and ROC government plans.

The U-2, a sleek, futuristic-looking airplane, was not designed to carry weapons. Only 49 feet long, with a wingspan of 80 feet, it weighed 17,270 pounds. At a cost of one million dollars, including development, the U-2 was considered the greatest aerospace bargain. Flying the plane was certainly a unique experience, but landing it was truly a challenge, even for seasoned pilots like Robin. The landing gear was unusual because, rather than the configuration of conventional aircraft with two front wheels under the nose and one under the tail, commonly called 'tail draggers', the U-2's landing gear was configured like a bicycle. The new landing gear was lighter which ultimately allowed for the weight of additional special equipment. Balancing the aircraft on the bicycle gear was especially tricky for takeoff and landing. The aircraft's range was 3,600 miles without refueling, almost the distance from New York to Los Angeles. The greatest feature of the U-2 was its ability to fly at altitudes greater than 70,000 feet. To fulfill its primary purpose, the U-2 was capable of collecting multi-sensor photographs, electro-optic, infrared and radar imagery.

Traditionally basic pilot training was conducted in two-seater aircraft with the instructor providing oversight as the student performed the required maneuvers. The instructor also graded the student as he performed the standard training curriculum. However, as Robin and his classmates soon learned, the U-2 was unlike any other aircraft. ROCAF General Hsiuh "Mike" Hua, wrote in *Air Power History*, Spring 2002, "There was no two-seater (U-2) available, so every pilot's first flight was solo." That meant students were required to learn flight procedures from lectures, books, manuals, cockpit schematics and students' own handwritten notes taken during class. However, due to the secret nature of the aircraft and its mission, removal of training aids from the classroom was prohibited and strictly enforced.

***

David Clark worked with a knitting company in Massachusetts in the 1930s. He left to start his own business manufacturing two-way stretch fibers used in women's girdles. Although his formal education ended at the age of 15 when he left school to work full time, at his father's insistence he attended evening courses in accounting and business. He earned no higher education after grammar school, but he maintained an insatiable interest in science. By the age of 39 he had been granted six patents for inventions related to the knitting industry.

Through his friend, E. J. Baldes, head of Biophysics at the Mayo Clinic, a world-renowned US medical facility, David Clark began research into the development of anti-gravity or 'G' suits as they were more commonly called. The suits required for flights above 65,000 feet were vital in saving a pilot's life if the aircraft lost pressure. Without a pressure suit to provide supplemental oxygen, the pilot had 60 seconds maximum before he became incapacitated due to decompression. During his research, Clark became acquainted with a

US Navy flight surgeon stationed on the aircraft carrier USS *Franklin Delano Roosevelt*. The flight surgeon asked him to design and manufacture an ear protection device for support personnel on the flight deck of the carrier. They had nothing but their hands covering their ears as protection from the deafening jet engine noise. Clark invented ear protectors for the Navy, and the design was so successful that other government agencies soon began purchasing the devices for their own flight personnel. Clark Company ear protectors are used by military and civilian pilots to this day. Through that contact, Clark pursued his production of the pressure suit, and the company began a blitz production for the Navy.

When the end of World War II arrived, the company anticipated an order from the Navy to cease production. However, the order was, in fact, just the opposite, and the Clark Company continued production. In 1946 the US Air Force became interested in the development of the pressure suit. The future of aviation had a special niche for the David Clark Company. With a budget of $20,000, the Air Force ordered 20 pressure suits from the Clark Company. Through much trial and error and reviews by Wright Patterson AFB, a final design was approved. With modifications over the years, the Clark Company has continued to manufacture pressure suits for US Air Force and Navy pilots as well as NASA astronauts. Like all US pilots, ROCAF pilots traveled to the David G. Clark Company in Worcester, Massachusetts to be measured for their custom fitted anti-gravity suits. Currently, the company has 12 standard sized patterns for the suits, with the exception of a few female astronauts who are now custom fitted due to their petite size.

One USAF pilot recalled his clandestine experience at the company. Instructed to travel to the David Clark Company without any military ID, the pilot was directed to wear civilian clothes only, and no GI issue underwear. He was met by a man who drove him to the Clark Company and handed him over to personnel there for the measuring process. The main floor of the Clark Company accommodated row upon row of sewing machines operated by women making bras and corsets, the original products of the company. The pilot was led to the basement area. In a small room at the end of a hall the pilot was told to remove all clothes except underwear and to stand on a two-foot high elevated platform. A stoop-shouldered elderly man with a tape measure draped around his neck then measured every inch of the pilot's body, absolutely every inch. After the measurement process, the pilot was released and told to return the next day. At that time, the pilot again stripped to his underwear and donned what appeared to be long underwear before the pressure suit. Company technicians helped hook everything correctly and instructed how the suit should be worn. Specialists pronounced the suit to be the correct fit and handed the pilot a bag with two pressure suits.

Most pilots had similar thoughts about the first time they wore the pressure suit with the extreme constricted fit, and ROCAF pilots were no exception. Most significant was the tight neck seal which was approximately five inches smaller than the pilot's neck size to ensure a very secure fit. Two Physiological Support technicians attached the pilot's faceplate to ensure it was sealed with absolutely no leaks. No one admitted to being claustrophobic in the pressure suit; thoughts of discomfort were soon dismissed with the importance of an impending mission to consider.

***

After only two weeks of classroom training, Robin sat in the cockpit of the U-2 for the first time. It was exciting to finally be in the driver's seat. The cockpit was extremely compact with every available inch of space housing the many dials, indicators and gauges. The instructor directed Robin to locate and identify each instrument while blindfolded and to explain its function. The second time in the cockpit, dressed in the regulation flight suit, Robin started the aircraft, taxied it a short distance and returned it to the ramp. He did not wear the pressure suit at that time because he was not flying at altitude. The next time he was ready for a real flight, with takeoff, two hours in the air and landing, while wearing the pressure suit. Robin felt in harmony with the aircraft as he put it through the maneuvers he learned in class; his confidence was buoyed with his success.

Landings in the U-2 were especially difficult due to its 80-foot wingspan and in-line gear. An experienced pilot and mechanic driving in a van called the 'mobile control' were stationed at the end of the runway and chased the aircraft once it was on final approach. The driver of the van pursued the aircraft, radioed the pilot in the cockpit, and advised the altitude he was flying for a safe landing. The goal was for the pilot to descend within one foot above the runway and hold until the engine stalled. Once the plane touched down and came to a stop, mechanics rushed to the aircraft. They grabbed the end of the wing to attach 'pogo wheels' that prevented the aircraft from tipping to one side due to the position of the unique landing gear. The pilot then taxied back to the ramp. The slightest breakdown in teamwork for this operation significantly compromised flight safety and could end in catastrophe.

Robin enjoyed the universal camaraderie of other pilots. He spent off-duty time at the Officers Club sharing and exchanging 'war stories' with his fellow pilots and the new American friends he had made. One story, passed along to each training class, he recalled occurred in Del Rio approximately 10 miles west of Laughlin AFB.

Local dairy farmer, Frank Gulick, awoke one day to learn that a U-2 had crashed in one of his pastures on the west side of town. Frank considered this an outstanding opportunity for an endless amount of local coffee shop chat, and he hurriedly drove to the pasture with his movie camera. To his surprise, as he was filming, US Air Force security officers and investigators arrived with weapons drawn, sealed the area of the downed aircraft and confiscated Frank's camera. Maybe the local citizens were not aware of the complexities of the U-2 and its mission, but the pilots definitely knew their roles and the sensitivity of the associated global politics.

Laughlin AFB maintained a recreation facility at nearby Lake Walk (later named Lake Amistad) where Robin and the ROCAF pilots joined USAF personnel boating and picnicking on weekends. He was even treated to a bullfight in nearby Cuidad Acuna, Mexico, a town directly across the Rio Grande from Del Rio. It was a unique experience he recalled with delight some 40 years later.

One hundred and fifty miles east, San Antonio was the closest city with a population of approximately 585,000. Just seven miles west of Laughlin AFB, the nearby town of Del Rio, population 25,000, had little in the way of industry or commerce in 1960. However, the town had maintained a long association with the USAF beginning in 1943 when the base was first commissioned. It was named for Lieutenant Jack T. Laughlin, the first casualty of the Second World War from the area. Some life-long friendships between base personnel and local residents were formed around church and school functions. Accustomed for years to sights and sounds of various military jets flying at all times of the day and night, citizens knew the U-2s were something different. It wasn't the usual training activity at Laughlin; however, most were unaware of the significance of the new mission there.

To emphasize the secret nature of their training experience, the ROCAF pilots learned the locals had been told they were Hawaiian. If they had ever spoken to one of the residents, it would have been quite obvious they were not Hawaiian. However, Robin and his fellow Taiwanese pilots had little contact with anyone off base. Very few people in the nearby community were aware the US was training the Taiwanese pilots, and that was exactly as the USAF wanted it.

Their introduction to American foods came from USAF families they met through their training, frequently families of their instructors. Mexican food, typical of the south Texas border area, took a bit of getting used to; the flavors and spices were quite different from those in Taiwan. But the ROCAF pilots were so charming that their American hosts had no idea it was not a favorite food choice. Invitations to join USAF families in their homes were an opportunity for the ROCAF pilots to meet the wives and children as well. It was often the children who introduced the ROCAF pilots to games popular with kids in the US.

For the Taiwanese pilots, the training experience was a combination of exposure to a new aircraft, new culture and for some most significantly, a new language. Chris Pocock states in *Dragon Lady, A History of the U-2* Spyplane, that "The Dragon Lady was a difficult aircraft for the best of pilots to master, let alone ... in a foreign language, where very little of the written material was translated. Some ... thought that the pilot's manual ... should be rendered into Mandarin, but this was never officially done. Even in this setting where understanding technical information was critical, the depth of the ROCAF pilots' cultural heritage was profound. For example, instructors would ask the students if they understood the point being made. The answer was always 'yes'. They could not bring themselves to reply with 'no' fearing disgrace, or worse, dishonor." To help improve their conversational English skills and understanding of American slang, a local school principal conducted weekly evening classes with the pilots.

4

Black Cat Squadron

In 1949 when the Communists seized power of the mainland, the Kuomintang (KMT) Nationalist Party collapsed. The PRC signed a Thirty Year Friendship Pact with the Soviet Union in 1950, and the remainder of the Nationalists retreated across the Strait to Taiwan. The economy in Taiwan was dismal as was the state of the ROCAF. To continue to monitor the PRC movements, the 12th Photographic Reconnaissance Squadron (PRS) maintained a photo lab at Taoyuan.

The US signed the Taiwan Defense Treaty with the ROC in 1954 to share the threat from the Communists in the Far East. Taiwan Defense Command was established and the US Navy 7th Fleet extended patrol to the Taiwan Strait. With help from the US Military Assistance and Advisory Group (MAAG), Taiwan successfully reconstructed its military capabilities. The priority was air superiority and photo reconnaissance along the Strait. ROCAF received a number of P-51s flown in the Second World War, but which required conversion to photo recon. Pilots were required to shoot pinpoint, strip, mosaic and dicing

Some of the original Black Cat Squadron pilots. Back row from left: General Lee, Lau, Colonel Shan, Major Chong and Major Huang. Front row from left: Manufacturer's Technical Representative, Colon Fang, Bob Erickson (Robin's instructor) and Colonel Tiger Wang. (Robin Yeh's collection)

photography. All this was extremely difficult, given the pilot was occupied flying the target in enemy territory without a viewfinder or drift sight.

With his U-2 training completed, Robin returned to the Republic of China in the early summer of 1963 and welcomed the mild temperatures of 55-60 degrees Fahrenheit. It was a beautiful island with ocean breezes most of the year. Robin was delighted to be reunited with his wife, Betty, and he quickly settled into a comfortable life. He and Betty lived in family housing at the air force base and had access to the base shuttle bus for transportation throughout the base.

In 1958 the ROC and the US reached an agreement to create the 35th Squadron, known as the Black Cat Squadron. Initially two U-2Cs were assigned to an isolated part of Taoyuan Air Base. The unit was created under the cover of a high altitude weather research for ROCAF. For added security and deniability, all US military and CIA personnel assigned to Detachment H were issued official documents and identification with false names and cover titles as Lockheed tech reps. Black Cat pilots and ground crew never knew their US counterparts' real names or titles or which company or agency they represented.

Robin was thrilled to be part of the elite Black Cat Squadron at Taoyuan Air Base. It was with a great deal of pride that he wore the Black Cat Squadron patch on his jacket and cap. His Squadron Commander, Colonel Lu Xiliang (Michael), was the first and longest serving leader of the famous group. Pilots reported to the squadron daily to learn when they were scheduled to fly and which aircraft they would be assigned. There was much preparation prior to a scheduled U-2 recon flight. In addition to required crew rest, Robin studied maps of the target area and checked with the weather office to learn what he could expect over the objective area.

Target priorities over mainland China were many: the PRC nuclear program and its rate of progress, potential and actual nuclear test sites, nuclear weapons delivery systems, such as aircraft and missile factories, air bases and missile launch sites. Shipyards and landing craft factories indicating a large build-up would spell a potential for invasion of Taiwan. Any other military facility would draw interest as a potential target area.

Twelve hours before his take-off time, Robin reported to the flight surgeon for a physical exam to ensure that he was fit to fly. He slept for eight hours to be fully rested for the strenuous mission. He ate a high protein meal for sufficient energy to sustain him for the nine to 10-hour flight. Pre-breathing 100 percent oxygen for one hour before the flight was a requirement to prevent hypoxia. A team of technicians from the Physiological Support Division assisted Robin in dressing for the flight. The suit actually consisted of four parts: first the comfort suit (similar to long underwear), then the pressure suit, the parachute and finally the helmet. With all the layers in place, bending and stooping were almost impossible. Suited up, he could have passed as a character in a science fiction movie. The many layers of the pressure suit and the discomfort and profuse sweating with little movement required the backup pilot to perform routine functions associated with pre-flight preparation.

Robin and Major Le Nan Ping teamed up to serve as backup for each other. The responsibilities of the backup pilot were significant, and there were no shortcuts. While Robin suited up and prepared for the flight, Ping conducted the pre-flight. The inspection included a check of all systems to ensure absolute safety of the coming flight.

Operational missions of the 35th Squadron were approved by presidents of the US and ROC prior to each U-2 flight. Robin flew his first operational U-2 mission, designated GRC-171 on August 30, 1963, a nine-hour aerial photography flight. The approved order

U-2 full pressure suit demonstrated by Major Yang. (Author's own collection)

had been delivered to the command post navigator who drew up the maps. At the mission and intelligence briefing conducted by the navigator, intelligence officer and weather officer, Robin learned the latest weather forecast for departure, en route, recovery and alternate/emergency landing bases. During the intelligence part of the briefing, a CIA officer identified where Robin could expect to encounter any MiG action. At that time he learned his flight route, traced on the map. The target was clearly identified with key points for camera start/stop. Unique abort codes, secret words that would be used for emergency instructions or recall, were issued at that time. The backup pilot also attended the briefing in the event the primary pilot was unable to fly the mission. Take-off time was planned for arrival over the target area at noon when the sun would be at the best angle for photographs.

Thirty minutes before takeoff, a crew van transported Robin, his portable oxygen supply and several technicians to his assigned aircraft on the ramp. When Ping was satisfied of the air worthiness of the aircraft, he signaled approval for Robin to board the aircraft. Technicians helped Robin up the ladder and into the cockpit. They connected straps, belts, hoses, cables and communications lines. Those tasks completed, Ping came up the ladder to discuss any final issues. With no other tasks to complete, technicians closed the cockpit and Robin was finally ready for taxi to the active runway. Once in position for take-off, he made a final check of his instruments. When cleared for take-off by the control tower, he pushed the throttle forward and within seconds catapulted into the blue skies over Taiwan. He crossed the closest point to the mainland at 70,000 feet altitude and climbed out to the east toward

Aerial view from the plane. (Xu Lin)

the sea. At 70,000 feet, he was able to see the curvature of the earth and the darkened sky at the outer limits of the atmosphere. The awesome sight filled him with an overwhelming feeling of isolation. Limited space in the cramped cockpit restricted movement of arms, hands, legs and feet. He shifted each extremity as frequently as possible, but his muscles still became stiff from lack of motion during the long flight.

Black Cat pilots acknowledged the importance of their missions and the risks they took on each flight. Hours in cramped cockpits, possible aircraft or system malfunction and the threat of surface to air missiles were only a few of the many dangers facing the pilots on each flight. Frequent PRC radio stations broadcast messages such as:

> Dear U-2 Pilots, stop risking your lives to sell secrets of your motherland to the American capitalists for blood money. The motherland welcomes you back. If you fly back with a U-2, we will reward you with eight thousand ounces of gold.

At the time, all ROCAF U-2 pilots had been born in Mainland China, and had immigrated to Taiwan when the Nationalists followed Chiang Kai-Shek. Like Robin's family, the ROCAF pilots were loyal to the Nationalist Party of General Chiang.

As directed in his pre-flight briefing, Robin performed recon tasks at pre-loaded coordinates on his maps and charts. Primary areas of interest were military installations along the southern Chinese coast from Fujian to Yunnan and a portion of North Vietnam.

Prior to each flight, technicians stocked the cockpit with water and juice. Tubes similar to toothpaste contained food choices such as applesauce and peaches, or the pilot was able to make his own favorite selection for the flight. However, at the end of the nine-hour flight, Robin was severely dehydrated and fatigued. After he landed and taxied to the ramp, the technicians disconnected his equipment and helped him out of the cockpit. Photo specialists were already removing the exposed film from the equipment bay as he was transported to the squadron debriefing to discuss equipment problems, intelligence and operations. Pilots were allowed recuperation time before flying again. He then had a mandatory 24 hours off duty and was not scheduled to fly again for at least 48 hours. High altitude flights took a physical toll. Due to the limited number of U-2 aircraft in the ROCAF inventory and the need for recovery time following a flight, pilots were not scheduled to fly every day. However, when he was not on crew rest or recovery, Robin flew the T-33 to maintain his flight proficiency.

The CIA took possession of the film canisters after each flight and immediately flew them to USAF Yakota AFB, Japan, for processing. Uncomfortable with relinquishing control of the photo interpretation, ROC officials suffered considerable consternation. They had done everything the US had asked of them, but still were not authorized to do the film interpretation.

In the spring of 1961, Edward Helsberg of Hycon Manufacturing Company of Monrovia, California, manufacturer of the U-2 camera, made a visit to the ROC. Following a tour of the processing center, Colonel Tsai asked him if there was any additional equipment needed to begin interpretation of the U-2 film. Colonel Tsai reminded Helsberg that it was the principal duty of the Night Owl Squadron to perform film processing of ROCAF missions. Helsberg did not respond; Colonel Tsai believed it was an ominous sign.

Helsberg made a subsequent visit to Taoyuan with a USAF officer from the 67th Recon Tech Squadron at Yakota. Also with Helsberg was a representative of Eastman Kodak Company. All three again toured the entire facilities of the Night Owl Squadron. At the end of the tour, the US visitors requested a meeting with General I Fu En which was arranged for the following day. At that meeting, Colonel Tsai asked again why the film was going to Japan when there were fully equipped facilities at Taoyuan to do the job. He was told firmly that all U-2 mission film taken by ROCAF must be shipped to the 67th RTS. Colonel Tsai, tongue in cheek, asked if they wanted training film also. The Americans were quick to respond that U-2 film required specialized equipment for processing, but the existing equipment at Taoyuan could be modified for processing U-2 training film only.

Weeks later the Kodak Company sent a tech rep to the Night Owl Squadron with a 70mm film processor for U-2 Tracker film. The requested modifications were completed to change all the rollers and adjustments. Night Owl Squadron personnel realized then just how complicated the job was going to be. The U-2 required specially manufactured aerial film, and carried two 6,000 foot rolls onboard the aircraft. The film processing required chemical replacement at precise levels, and attention to tracking levels, speed, and temperature. With experience, the Night Owl Squadron gained proficiency. The Kodak tech rep was assigned a desk in the lab to monitor the film processing practice and provide oversight and technical assistance.

Robin's second U-2 flight, GRC-178 on September 26, 1963, went as planned, and he photographed areas over China's southern coast, as well as a small portion of North Vietnam during the 11-hour flight. Most significant was his photograph of Beijing at an oblique angle. The city was not politically important, but the more interesting atomic and missile facilities in the southwest suburb of Beijing were the primary targets for this mission.

In 1963 the ROC and the US were alerted to PRC nuclear facilities. On September 25 the Mission Photo Intelligence Report covered the Lanzhou diffusion plant and

Aerial view of Black Cat Squadron, Taoyuan Air Base. (Xu Lin)

surrounding area. It was a large compound assumed to be camouflaged into the mountains northeast of Lanzhou City and north of the Yellow River. A small number of houses were identified inside the compound, possibly housing for support personnel. According to intelligence reports, the Lanzhou plant was capable of producing enriched uranium, similar to the Manhattan Project of Oak Ridge, Tennessee.

His third and final flight, GRC-184 on November 1, 1963, marked his 30th birthday and was 18 days before his first wedding anniversary. Mission planners had designated Lanzhou as his target over Mainland China. Preparations for the flight were the same as previous flights, and again, Ping assisted as back up pilot. Robin followed the coordinates on his map and set up the cameras at the designated marks on his map. He flew the mission as planned, and easily identified the targets.

Ten hours into the flight at an altitude of 74,000 feet, the sun was low on the horizon. It was the last leg of his flight with the coast of the ROC in sight. Suddenly the System 12 radar detector, a red button on the instrument panel commonly known as the 'Oh S**t' indicator, sounded an audible alarm to signal his aircraft was targeted by a surface-to-air missile. Even with immediate evasive action as he had been trained, the left wing separated on contact and the canopy jettisoned as the cockpit instantly decompressed. The aircraft went into a nosedive and Robin was ejected from the cockpit.

Free falling, he fought to position himself to safely open his parachute. He learned in training, in the event of a high altitude bail-out, never attempt to open the parachute until at 20,000 feet or lower. Parachutes were designed to open automatically at 16,500 feet. Opening the parachute at a higher altitude could cause a blow out of several panels resulting

Aerial view over China of surface-to-air missile site. (Xu Lin)

Aerial view of Tiananmen Square in China. (Xu Lin)

in faster than normal rate of descent and a hard landing. Additionally, emergency oxygen could run out before reaching a lower altitude. Most critical was the opening shock could result in severe injury if the parachute straps were not in place and tightened properly.

He was alarmed to see the widening of the Yangtze River indicating his rapid descent as he plummeted to earth. With the river as a gauge of his altitude, he pulled the parachute cord and slowed his descent. Activity on the ground was visible from his altitude, and he identified a number of farms. The quiet of his descent allowed sounds on the ground, a truck and farm machinery. He maneuvered himself to a hillside near the town of Hsiang Yao as early evening approached. Little did he realize that the decision he made to open his parachute would be the last one he would make for himself for many years.

Aware of the diminishing daylight, he landed on the hillside, dazed and disoriented. In his confusion, Robin was unable to determine the extent of his injuries, but he felt extreme pain in his legs. Maybe he had not lost his legs in the rapid exit from the cockpit, a fear all pilots experience upon ejection. He was only semi-conscious when members of the Chinese People's Liberation Army Air Force (PLAAF) arrived and took him into custody. The Army had tracked his parachute from the crippled aircraft, and they drove near the area where he landed. They could not drive their truck to the site where he descended, and he could not walk due to his injuries. Soldiers scoured the nearby area and located a ladder to use as a stretcher to carry him down the hill where the truck waited to take him to a military hospital for treatment. Once doctors examined his injuries, they removed 59 fragments of shrapnel in his legs, treated and stitched his wounds. He remained in the hospital where a nurse came daily to check his wounds and change bandages. She told him he was to be discharged from the hospital soon. When he asked where he would go, the nurse replied, "The People's Liberation Army will take care of you."

A few days later his captors decided he had regained his strength sufficiently, and the wounds were healing well. He was issued a Mao suit that everyone wore at the time, long sleeve shirt, pajama style pants, tennis shoes and baseball cap. The suit looked faded and frayed, possibly even worn by someone else, but he had no choice.

Dressed in his standard issue uniform, Robin was repulsed by it as much as he had first admired Warren's Air Force uniform. He recalled the pride he felt with Black Cat patches on his own uniform. The PRC issued summer and winter uniforms, the winter one being only a slightly heavier version of the same style. Winter temperatures frequently dropped to 20 degrees Fahrenheit. A short jacket worn over his uniform would be his only protection from the severe elements. Three uniformed men came to his hospital room, one with different insignia who appeared to be the leader of the group. He was most likely an officer by appearance of his uniform; the other two men wore very plain uniforms with no insignia.

The leader introduced himself as Kuo, Section Chief of the Political Department of the PLAAF. There was no small talk or query about his health. Kuo announced they were transferring him to another facility. Robin was weak and still in pain from his wounds. Soldiers helped him into a transport van where he was seated on a bench between them. Each bump over the poorly maintained roads caused more pain and discomfort. When Robin asked where they were going, one of the soldiers replied, "To the Air Force Hostel." He asked where the Air Force Hostel was located, but there was no response from either of the soldiers. The term military hostel frequently denoted a place of lodging, a small hotel where traveling military soldiers stayed when on temporary assignment. While the hostel was on a military compound, it was unlike any he had ever been assigned.

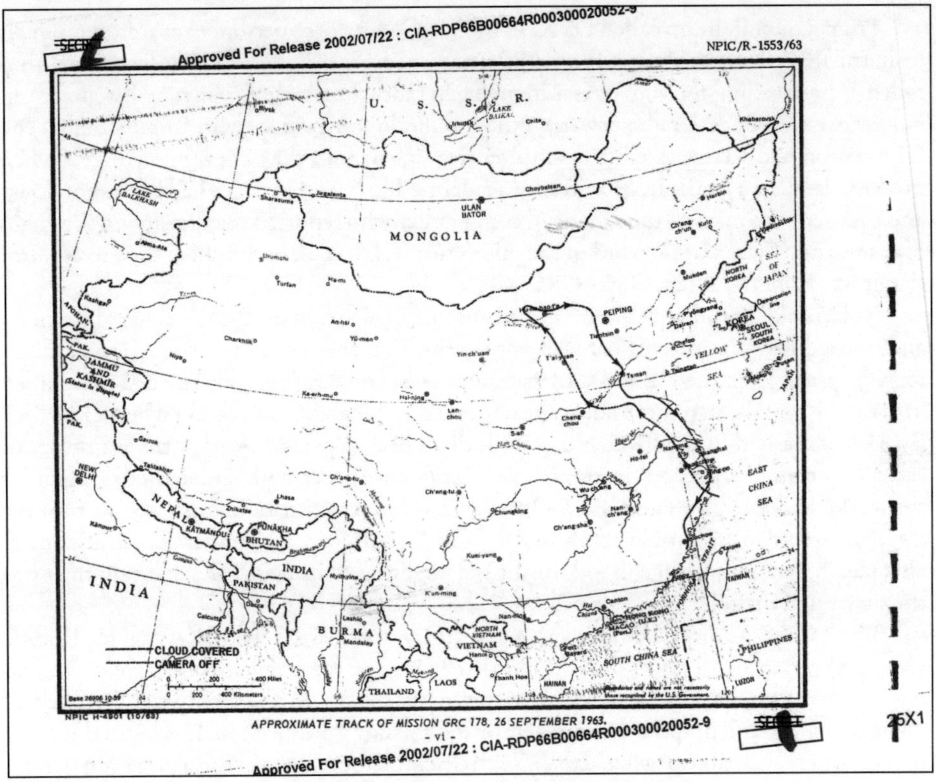

Map of Robin's flight. (Neal E. Coltrane)

He learned soon enough the accommodations were anything but comfortable. It was part of a compound surrounded by brick walls. Robin was escorted to a small room with single bed, small table and chair, all of which appeared very old and in poor condition. A toilet and sink completed the accessories of the room. A curtain covered the glass window in the door on the outside; the guards could watch whenever they wanted. With the curtain in place, he could not see out to the hall. One window with bars allowed him a view of the roofs of houses outside the compound. Trees were visible above the compound wall. In the quiet stillness of his room, he heard outside noises; voices sounded like a distinct Beijing accent. Though he was not informed of his location, he concluded he must be in the Beijing area.

In the solitude of his cell, Robin had much time to ponder his situation. Was he a political pawn between the PRC and the ROC? Would the PRC keep him in prison for the rest of his life? The questions haunted him and compounded his helplessness. He knew it was unlikely he would get honest answers from his captors. *The Selected Works of Mao Tse Tung* consisting of four volumes held the centerpiece on the table. A newspaper dated November 18, 1963 was also on the table. With sadness, Robin recalled this date as his and Betty's first anniversary, and their plans to celebrate the event when he returned home.

A doctor came to the hostel daily to check his wounds. She said he was recovering well. There was no idle conversation as sometimes occurs between doctor and patient. He thanked her, but she appeared indifferent to his gratitude.

From a mountaintop called Da Xi in the ROC, Air Force personnel monitored signals from the PRC. It was common for the PRC to broadcast directly to a pilot by name. "Your father is here calling for you," was a frequent broadcast message for anyone listening. On November 1, 1963, the radio tower on the mountain lost contact with Robin's flight. The CIA station had a large satellite dish to receive signals, and they knew immediately when the PRC launched a missile. Monitors were alarmed to hear that a U-2 had been shot down, and they sent the news to the squadron commander who reported the disaster up the chain of command. There was no word of the pilot's survival. It took only a short time to confirm that it was Robin's aircraft, Flight GRC-184.

Robin's older brother, Warren, then a lieutenant colonel in the ROCAF, heard the news and pressed his own internal contacts for details. But, there was no information at all on Robin's status. Even the US and CIA had no way to know for certain if he had been killed in the crash, or if he had survived. Warren recalled an incident years earlier when a ROCAF F-101 had crashed in the PRC and the pilot had been captured. At that time, a notice of the pilot's capture appeared in the *People's Daily* newspaper with circulation throughout the world. However, the crash of a U-2 was a very different situation. First, no one thought a surface-to-air missile could reach its target at 74,000 feet. If the aircraft was at a lower altitude, there was more likelihood the missile might reach its mark. The question then was the survival of the pilot.

Black Cat Squadron Commander, Colonel Lu, was alerted that the signal for Robin's U-2 had been lost. All pilots understood that flying the spy plane involved great risk and few ever bailed out safely. Colonel Lu deeply regretted the responsibility that he faced to tell Robin's wife and his parents, of the crash and missing status. Colonel Lu located Robin's parents where they were playing *mahjong* with friends. The congenial social occasion quickly turned to a sad time for all present. According to history of similar situations, the pilot's status was simply listed as 'missing'.

Wei-Shen never contemplated the idea that his son could have been captured alive; but Shi-Wueng had a 'sixth sense' about the event. She insisted he was alive, and over the years, she held firmly to that belief. Her devout Buddhist belief sustained her. In 1963, all Robin's siblings were pursuing their own careers and living in different parts of the world. Robin's brother, Steve, taught in a school in Hong Kong. No one had contacted him to soften the news; he read in the newspaper the report of a U-2 shoot down over the PRC. The only publicized news reported that Robin's plane had been shot down; there was nothing about the survival of the pilot. He was simply presumed dead. Steve was stunned by the news.

Grief overwhelmed Steve to the point he didn't even want to speak to anyone. With no bereavement leave, he had to work or not be paid. It was impossible for him to concentrate and properly lecture his classes during that time. Instead, he instructed his students to do practice exercises while he continued to grieve. Robin's brother, Creek, experienced similar emotional devastation. Each of the other brothers and sisters coped as well as they could, but also believed him to be dead.

After six months passed without word from the pilot or the Communist Chinese, a missing ROCAF pilot was officially declared dead. Such would be the case of Robin Yeh. The ROCAF was so certain of Robin's demise that after only four months had elapsed, on March 29, 1964, the ROC honored all its fallen Air Force heroes at a memorial ceremony. On that occasion Robin's name was included in the memorial and a gravestone marking his death was set in a designated place of honor. Although his mother had been told he

~~SECRET~~
NO FOREIGN DISSEM

Approved For Release 2000/08/04 : CIA-RDP78B04560A001800010029-8

NPIC/R-1553/63

City, Installation	Coordinates	WAC	Installation Numbers BE	Installation Numbers NPIC
PARTIALLY COMPLETED SA-2 SAM SITE. SIX LAUNCH POSITIONS UNOCCUPIED. OBLIQUITY PRECLUDES FURTHER INTERPRETATION. 25X1D [redacted]				
AIR INSTALLATIONS			25X1A	
KUEI-SUI AIRFIELD EAST 5.5 NM ENE OF KUEI-SUI. 4,980 X 190 FT ENE/WSW RUNWAY, SERVICEABLE. THE EASTERN 4,350 FT PORTION OF RUNWAY IS PROBABLY PIERCED STEEL-PLANK SURFACE AND THE WESTERN 630 FT EXTENSION IS PROBABLY GRADED-EARTH. A SECOND RUNWAY, 3,300 [redacted] FT E/W DIRT STRIP IS UNSERVICEABLE. 25X1D NO APPARENT CHANGE IN FACILITIES SINCE [redacted] 25X1D [redacted] EXCEPT NO HANGAR OBSERVED. 25X1D AIRCRAFT -- NONE OBSERVED. 25X1D [redacted]	4051N 11148E	0288	[redacted]	7-B
PEIPING AIRFIELD CENTRAL 13 NM NE OF PEIPING. APPROXIMATELY 9,200 X 300 FT N/S CONCRETE RUNWAY, SERVICEABLE. FACILITIES INCLUDE PARALLEL LOOP TAXIWAY WITH 3 CROSSOVER LINKS, LARGE TERMINAL AND EXTENSIVE PARKING FACILITIES ON WEST SIDE OF FIELD, AND PROBABLE POL AND SUPPORT FACILITIES SW OF FIELD. OBLIQUITY PRECLUDES FURTHER INTERPRETATION. AIRCRAFT -- APPROXIMATELY 30 UNIDENTIFIED. 25X1D [redacted]	4004N 11635E	0289	[redacted]	34
CHANG-PING AIRFIELD 7 NM SE OF CHANG-PING.	4009N 11619E	0289	[redacted]	3

2

~~SECRET~~
NO FOREIGN DISSEM

Approved For Release 2000/08/04 : CIA-RDP78B04560A001800010029-8

Description of Robin's flight from declassified US documents. (Neal E. Coltrane)

~~SECRET~~
NO FOREIGN DISSEM

Approved For Release 2000/08/04 : CIA-RDP78B04560A001800010029-8

NPIC/R-1553/63

City, Installation	Coordinates	WAC	Installation Numbers BE	Installation Numbers NPIC
6,200 X 180 FT NW/SE CONCRETE RUNWAY, SERVICEABLE. FACILITIES INCLUDE LOOP TAXIWAY WITH 30 HARDSTANDS, 2 CONNECTING LINKS, LARGE PARKING APRON WITH 3 HANGARS SITUATED CENTRALLY ON TAXIWAY, LARGE SUPPORT AREA WITH BARRACKS, ADMINISTRATIVE BUILDINGS AND STORAGE FACILITIES SW OF FIELD, SECURED AMMUNITION STORAGE AREA WITH 10 STORAGE AND 5 SUPPORT BUILDINGS IMMEDIATELY SW OF NW END OF FIELD, AND PEIPING SAM SITE B-35 IMMEDIATELY OFF NNW END OF FIELD. AIRCRAFT -- 14 UNIDENTIFIED STRAIGHT-WING PROBABLE TRANSPORT AND 21 PROBABLE AIRCRAFT. 25X1D [redacted]			25X1A	
CHI-NAN AIRFIELD 3.5 NM WNW OF CHI-NAN. 7,100 X 210 FT N/S CONCRETE RUNWAY WITH 1,200 FT SOD OVERRUN AT SOUTH END AND 800 FT SOD OVERRUN AT NORTH END, SERVICEABLE. 3,900 X 325 FT NNE/SSW PREPARED SURFACE RUNWAY WITH 980 X 165 FT PREPARED SURFACE EXTENSION AT NNE END (TOTAL LENGTH 4,880 FT), SERVICEABLE. FACILITIES INCLUDE N/S TAXIWAY WITH 2 CROSSOVER LINKS CONNECTING WITH CONCRETE RUNWAY, ONE CONCRETE PARKING APRON, 17 REVETTED HARDSTANDS ADJACENT TO TAXIWAY, AND AN ALERT APRON AT BOTH ENDS OF CONCRETE RUNWAY. TWO PARKING APRONS ON SSW END OF GRADED EARTH RUNWAY. HANGAR FACILITY WITH APRON, STORAGE BUNKERS, AND BARRACKS AT SW END OF INSTALLATION. AIRCRAFT -- 44 FAGOT/FRESCO, 7 COLT, ONE	3641N 11655E	0381	[redacted]	69-A

3

~~SECRET~~
NO FOREIGN DISSEM

Approved For Release 2000/08/04 : CIA-RDP78B04560A001800010029-8 was missing and presumed dead, she refused to believe it and would not go to the gravesite, continuing to hold firm to her belief that he was alive.

5

Captured and Confined

The squeaky lock on his cell door unlatched and a soldier ordered him to dress quickly to meet the political officers waiting to see him. Robin was escorted to another room and seated at a table. Kuo, the officer he met when he was discharged from the hospital, appeared to be in charge. Kuo demanded, "Why are you flying here?" Robin studied the faces of his interrogators, men about his own age with steely eyes and dressed in the uniform of the People's Liberation Army. Robin responded as he had been trained with only his name, rank and serial number.

Kuo spoke with authority, "The People's Republic already knows all about you." The officer then related specific information about Robin's personal and professional history that was surprisingly accurate. They knew his father's name and occupation, his mother's name, and his brother, Warren's occupation in the ROCAF. Robin was ordered to write the names of people he knew in the ROCAF after which his captors double checked their sources to ensure he was telling the truth. It troubled him that they had so much personal information about him and his family. Who did he know would pass such information to the Communists? Were they able to get this information from listening devices? It was certainly disturbing to learn. One of the three men at the table recorded the interrogation with pen and paper.

Kuo interrogated, "What was your mission?" Robin responded, "I do not know." And he really did not. Based on the security 'need to know' requirements, he was given only sufficient information to perform his flight. Anything beyond that was someone else's responsibility to put the pieces of the puzzle together. The interrogator became angry and asked, "Why you don't know the target? How can you take pictures?" Robin patiently answered, "I follow the information on the maps saying when to turn on the cameras." He remembered the old Chinese saying: "The more you say, the more you lose." He decided to provide as little information as he could and stick to the same story at each interview. He did know most of the targets, but he wisely decided to withhold that information to avoid more questions. It seemed inconceivable to the interrogators that Robin would not know all the details of his own flight.

Kuo shot out more rapid-fire questions: "Who planned your mission? Were they Chinese or American? Was the CIA involved?" Robin replied patiently, "They were Chinese." "What were their names?" demanded the interrogator. "Sun and Yang" replied Robin. "No Americans planned the flight?" they asked. "There was an American advisor, but I do not know his name." Many of Robin's answers were the same, "I don't know."

The interrogator became frustrated and began to yell loudly. They verbally assaulted him with a barrage of anti-Nationalist propaganda, and they reminded him that he would one day confess to them. Kuo summoned guards to return Robin to his cell and admonished, "You don't know our policy. Our great leader Chairman Mao taught us 'lenient treatment to those who confess frankly, severe punishment to those who remain stubborn, reward to those who provide helpful information.'"

The confrontations with the political officers came at regular intervals, two officers twice a week. Following the previous interrogation, Robin was brought to the same room. Zhang stated he was in charge in Kuo's absence. Each time they came Robin asked, "When can I return to the ROC?" Early on he was told that most pilots only stayed about 10 months then returned to the ROC. Still, Robin could not recall a single similar situation he had heard about since he had been a member of the ROCAF. However, the news from his captors filled him with a little hope, and Robin concentrated on maintaining a positive attitude to get him through this ordeal. He thought of Betty often in those days and felt she, too, was a victim of his tragedy. Robin could only imagine what she must be experiencing and was saddened by the powerlessness of his situation.

Zhang began the day's session on a more pleasant note with a common greeting. He asked when Robin reported to the U-2 squadron, where he learned to fly the U-2 and what previous missions he had flown. "According to our records," Zhang revealed, "each time our surface-to-air missile's guidance radar is turned on, the U-2 evaded the missile site. How did pilots know they were near the missile site?" Robin responded, "I have explained before that pilots work on 'need to know' basis. I don't know what other pilots did. We did not know about other missions than our own."

It was at that moment that Robin recalled he had been ejected from the cockpit before he pressed the red button to activate the detonator in the equipment bay to destroy all the electronics. He considered that it was possible the PRC had found the System 12 in his aircraft wreckage and were able to determine its function. He decided not to deny the existence of the System 12 fearing the PRC could catch him in a lie.

Zhang conducted the next session and asked mostly about operations of the RF-101 which Robin flew prior to being assigned to the U-2 squadron. While he was assigned to the RF-101 squadron, Robin recalled a pilot, Major Wu Paotze, who was shot down and captured in August 1961. He survived and later broadcast over Communist radio calling RF-101 pilots by name to join him and bring a RF-101. Wu said in his broadcast that he had been treated well, but ROCAF believed it to be due to the Communists' brainwashing. This part of the interrogation was of little concern to Robin because he figured the PRC knew all about the RF-101 from Wu.

Zhang showed Robin two photos and asked where they were taken. One photo looked to be taken at a dance party with wives or girlfriends present. It was maybe at the home of one of the squadron officers. Zhang asked for the names of the pilots in the photo. Robin knew most of them except those who came after he left the squadron. The second photo was obviously a cookout with a number of people around a swimming pool. Robin recognized many of the tech reps as well as Colonel Lu, Lieutenant Colonel Pao and Lieutenant Colonel Yang. Most were relaxing around the pool, some held drinks. Robin told Zhang he recognized the Chinese in the photo, the Americans present were advisors. He reported he did not know the Americans' names because he had little contact with them. Zhang told Robin the PRC knew the names of all the people in the photo and read the Chinese names. Robin suspected Zhang did not know how to read names in English, his reason for omitting the Americans in the photo.

During a subsequent meeting, Zhang brought Communist reading material, the most significant, Mao Tse-Tung's *Little Red Book*. Zhang said, "You must read Chairman Mao's book. We will discuss it with you." They finally explained the rules: "You are not permitted to go outside without a guard, and you must not speak to anyone." Although Robin spoke the Mandarin Chinese dialect they were speaking, they told him he did not speak like the population there. Robin had always addressed people as Mr. or Mrs. as a sign of respect, but he was told the appropriate form of address applied to everyone now was simply 'Comrade'. He noticed that in the time he had been confined, he had not seen a single person with even a slight smile or happy face.

Robin was eventually allowed outside his room with a guard who was like a shadow. His daily routine was very structured and seldom varied. Each morning before breakfast, he walked with his guard to a park a block away. The wounds on his legs were healing, and he wanted to stay fit. He ran in the park and exercised for approximately one hour. His guard then summoned him to return to the hostel for his breakfast. Meals were on a strict schedule: breakfast at 7:30 a.m., lunch at 11:30 a.m. and the evening meal at 6:00 p.m. Breakfast consisted of porridge, a dish of peanuts and a bowl of pickles. Lunch was a small portion of meat with a few vegetables. The evening meal was similar to lunch. All his meals were delivered to his room from the Officers Mess Hall at the nearby military facility and were significantly better than food consumed by the average Chinese citizen at that time.

After breakfast, Robin was required to listen to the morning Communist Party radio news for one hour. Following the radio news, he studied Mao's *Little Red Book*. In the afternoon he read newspapers and studied books about the history of the Communist Party. This schedule of activity was routinely considered 'brain washing' procedures for the POW. However, Robin and his family had been supporters of a democracy for many years, and the Communist doctrine was impossible to accept.

The interrogations ceased with no explanation; Robin considered maybe Zhang ran out of questions or there were no new answers. When interrogations resumed, the intervals between sessions became longer. The questions were a rehash of the previous ones. With nothing to occupy his mind, Robin spent time in his cell lying on his bed watching the sky through the window. The weather changed drastically at times from bright blue sky above to strong gusts of wind to cold air with frost on neighboring rooves. The wounds on his legs had healed, but the scars itched often. There was no medication or herbal remedy to help the itching. With nothing to do, he waited and waited.

A month later, Kuo returned to continue interrogations. At this time, a theme began to emerge; Kuo was interested in knowing about the Americans in the squadron. He announced, "If you want to go back to Taiwan to unite with your family, we will let you go after the investigation is completed. In the meantime, I want you to learn how much the Communist Party has accomplished and how much life in the mainland has been improved." Ever alert, Robin asked respectfully, "Held in this small room, how can I see the great work your party has accomplished?" Kuo reminded Robin that they provided the *Liberation Army Daily*. Robin was instructed to read the newspaper and write his comments for Zhang to criticize as instruction and appreciation of the Communist Party.

The *Liberation Army Daily* was not a newspaper in the true sense that reports of events were chronicled there. It was an additional means of indoctrination, and Robin lost interest reading it. At the end of the interrogation, Kuo asked if Robin had anything else to say. Robin acknowledged, "I know the Communist Party has treated me well, but the weather is getting colder and these clothes are not enough for the coming winter." Kuo instructed Zhang to immediately take care of that, and a week later Zhang returned with heavy clothes and daily necessities. Zhang told Robin, "Chairman Mao has taught us to treat prisoners of war well. You are to be provided for as if you are a junior member of the party. You will receive a little Chinese currency (slightly more than one US dollar) each month. I will keep the money for you, and if you need anything, I will send a soldier to buy it for you."

In December 1963 as he read the newspaper, Robin was surprised to see a story awarding a medal to the commander of the missile battalion responsible for shooting down his U-2. The report mentioned the location of the wreckage, but nothing about the pilot. He had hoped the newspaper would report the pilot had been captured alive, and quoted in the newspaper in Hong Kong. If that was the case, maybe his wife or his parents would know he was alive. Sadly, there was not even the slightest mention of the pilot.

In the Southeast Asia country of Vietnam, a few thousand miles south of Robin's location, war was in full swing between the Communists of the North and the democratic South Vietnam. However, there was no reference to the conflict in the newspapers Robin was required to read. The Chinese Communists tightly controlled all news media and reported mostly domestic issues of their choosing, certainly no information about anything outside the PRC.

Gradually the tension between Robin and the guards relaxed, and he began speaking with the younger soldier named Wang who was only 18 years old. He spoke a few words when Wang delivered meals. Breakfast was sometimes corn grits or porridge and sometimes pickles. At noon the main meal of the day was often steamed buns or rice with greens or tofu. The evening meal was rice porridge or noodle soup. On Chinese New Year's Day, the main meal was a veritable feast compared to most days. For the special day, Robin was served boiled dumplings with meat and vegetables which was the first meal he had actually enjoyed since his capture.

Following the New Year's feast, Robin spoke to Wang, "The dumplings were very good. Did you enjoy them?" Wang said, "We soldiers dine in the mess hall. Your food is provided by the small kitchen for the political officers. Your food is better than ours. We eat mainly meals from corn or sorghum. Rice or a bun is a special treat." Robin said, "Even with these meals, I feel hungry before the next meal." Wang responded, "I don't think you know real hunger," Wang responded. He told Robin the area where he lived was in a western province. Food was always scarce before the harvest season, and people had to eat grass roots or even tree bark to survive. Famine spread throughout China in 1961. Wang joined the Army when he learned the Communists treated soldiers better than civilians.

Wang told Robin people in China were grateful to have Chairman Mao providing food for them, unlike people in Taiwan who had only banana peels to eat. Robin was greatly amused by Wang's statement, and he stumped the young soldier by asking, "If everybody eats the banana peels, where does the banana flesh go?" The next day Wang was replaced by another soldier who was able to recognize the line between revolutionaries and counter-revolutionaries. Through the small window in the door of his cell, Robin knew they watched his every move. Guards were rotated at least monthly.

The suffocating summer heat made the cell even more oppressive. When the soldier brought his evening meal with the *Liberation Army Daily*, Robin read the headlines with interest. The newspaper reported that the PRC shot down another of Chiang Kai Shek's bandits. Somewhat certain it was a U-2, Robin wondered about the pilot's survival. A few days later, Kuo brought a gold ring which Robin recognized immediately. It was Le Nan Ping's wedding ring which he wore all the time. The name engraved inside was Le's wife, Yeh Chiuying. Robin was close with Le's family before his own marriage to Betty. Kuo asked if Robin knew who owned such a ring. Robin answered, "It belongs to my colleague, Le Nan

Ping. Is he the pilot of the downed aircraft?" Kuo said he could not answer that question.

Robin recognized the quality of his meals had improved, maybe a sign the autumn harvest had been plentiful. He had been incarcerated now for almost a year. The newspaper devoted a great deal of coverage to the Fifteenth National Anniversary of the People's Republic of China. Preparations were underway for a celebration.

When Zhang met with Robin now, there were few questions, but more indoctrination. After one such meeting with Kuo, Robin asked, "When can I return to Taiwan? I would like to reunite with my wife and parents."

"We have not heard any favorable comments regarding your case." "Confined in my room all day, how can I appreciate all that you have accomplished?" Robin asked. "Did you not read the newspaper that tells you all the good deeds?"

Robin had quick responses for Kuo. "The news is all so good. It is hard to believe it is not exaggerated." Two weeks later Zhang ordered Robin to pack his belongings and prepare for a transfer to a hostel in Beijing. Robin asked Zhang, "Why do I move there?" "I don't know. It is an order." After a year confinement, Robin felt a bit wiser, but there was no way to predict what was next in store for him.

A black van drove him, Zhang and another soldier to a house inside a gated compound. He was turned over to a soldier named Zhao then Zhang departed. Robin was led to a room slightly larger than the previous room where he spent his first year. The ever present red cover book, *The Selected Works of Mao Zedong*, held the centerpiece on the small table. Another red book, *Quotations of Chairman Mao*, was only the size of his hand. Robin figured it was small to enable followers to carry it with them. In this room, he could hear a broadcast from a distant loudspeaker. After reporting news, instruction and indoctrination from the county government, listeners were treated to revolutionary songs. When he was brought to the main room of the house, he was ordered to bow in front of a photo of Chairman Mao. He complied with the direction.

Shortly after New Year's Day 1965, the newspaper ran a story of another ROCAF U-2 shot down over Inner Mongolia. As with the previous news reports there was no mention of the survival of the pilot. Two months later, another RF-101 was shot down by a MiG-19 in Guangdong Province. The pilot, Chang Yupao, was reported killed. Robin observed the PRC treated U-2 and RF-101 pilots differently. There was never any mention of the pilot of a downed U-2, but there were always reports in detail about the crashed RF-101. There might be political value for the U-2 pilots because the aircraft was a joint project with the ROC and the US; the RF-101 was a project of the ROC only. Robin recalled that the PRC maintained a diplomatic channel open with the US through Poland since the Korean cease-fire in 1953. However, if the PRC had not reported to Taiwan that Robin was alive, negotiations would never commence.

In the spring of 1965, Kuo came to the house to meet Robin. Robin greeted Kuo, "I haven't seen you for quite some time. How have you been?" Kuo explained that Chairman Mao declared the nation should learn from the People's Liberation Army, and the political department was sending teams to schools, industries and communes to teach Mao's doctrine. Kuo told Robin, "I am glad to hear you have been studying Chairman Mao's publications and the *Little Red Book*."

Kuo did not agree with all of Robin's interpretations, but he was glad to see an attitude change which he thought was a good sign. Robin found many statements in Mao's books totally unacceptable to him. Many of the statements were inconsistent and vague in meaning which could be interpreted to suit the reader. At the end of their conversation, Kuo told Zhao, "I think you can take Yeh to see some movies or show him the progress in town when you have time." Robin was happy to have a chance to be away from the detention house and be outside in the fresh air.

Cinema was introduced in China in 1896 with the first film, *The Battle of Dingjunshan*, produced in 1905. At the time, the film industry was centered in Shanghai. In 1931, the first sound film produced, *Sing-Song Girl Red Peony*. Later in the 1930s the conflict between the Nationalists and Communists was reflected in films of the period. Following the Communist revolution in 1949, earlier films and foreign movies were banned. During the Cultural Revolution, the film industry almost came to a standstill from 1967 to 1972.

Zhao arranged an evening to take Robin to a nearby movie theater. Accompanied by another soldier, Robin and Zhao walked to the theater. The interior was no surprise; it was quite old and in a state of disrepair. The air inside the theater was thick with cigarette smoke. They sat together in the back row with Robin between the two soldiers. As they talked, a man turned from the row in front of them to stare. Likely his attention was drawn by Robin's southern accent. One of the soldiers quickly yelled at the man who turned back in his seat and paid no further attention to them.

The movie would be considered a third rate film by Western standards, the theme being revenge against capitalist exploitation. Unlike movies in the ROC or US, this one was not really for entertainment; it was another source of indoctrination and propaganda. Shouted slogans in the movie were part of the script with attendees participating in the melee.

Wreckage from four U-2 crashes was collected and reassembled in front of the Military Museum of the Chinese People's Revolution. It was easy to see the four had been aircraft, but details were difficult to visualize. Zhao brought Robin to see the exhibition. Lines for entrance were long, and once at the front of the line, they were not allowed to go near the aircraft. They overheard a disappointed spectator say, "What a waste of time. Are these really the U-2 spy airplanes? If they did shoot down these aircraft, where are the pilots?" Robin said nothing but seeing the wreckage of his own aircraft was a poignant moment for him.

On a cool, crisp autumn day, Zhao and another soldier took Robin to tour the National Museum of History located east of Tiananmen Square, the Palace of Emperors. Zhao reported proudly the square could hold half a million people. On this day there were only a few milling about. The Great Hall of People contained an auditorium with 10,000 seats and 29 conference rooms named for each of the provinces of China. He was greatly impressed with the size of the structure. Maybe the Communist Party had accomplished something special for the country, but it was a small contribution considering the basic needs of the country. Inside the museum, Robin was shocked to learn the PRC had re-written history showing they had won the war against Japan, rather than General Chiang Kai-Shek's Nationalists. Robin had a clear memory of the eight years when millions of Chinese civilians were massacred during the Japanese invasion. He also remembered the Japanese armed forces deployed in China had surrendered to the KMT government, not the other way around. The PRC could not bring themselves to credit the Nationalists for anything.

After New Year in 1966, political unrest was simmering. Newspapers and broadcasts began using new political terms: capitalist-roader, revisionist, ox-devil, snake-demon, Cultural Revolution, etc. In the spring, the Great Proletarian Cultural Revolution was implemented. The Red Guards organized in schools, and teachers and school administrators were the first to be criticized and humiliated in public.

In September, after a long absence, Kuo and Zhao came to meet with Robin. Kuo had been promoted and given more responsibilities. Robin made an appeal for release once again. He said, "It has been three years since I have been confined to this small room. When can I return to Taiwan to see my wife and parents?" He read of Gary Powers' release from Russia, and pointed out that he was released after less than two years in prison. Kuo told Robin once again to be patient, "All the political officers are very busy. You do know the Great Proletarian Cultural Revolution is in full swing now?" He told Robin of a forthcoming rally in Tiananmen Square, and ordered Zhao to get a permit for Robin to see the event.

Three weeks later, in the early pre-dawn hours, Zhao and another soldier hurried Robin into a waiting jeep. They stopped at the side door of a building, and entered where guards checked permit documents. Granted permission to enter, they climbed the stairs to the second floor where they saw through a window all of Tiananmen Square completely populated with people from one side to the other. They looked very young and all wore red armbands with Red Guard written in gold. Handwritten posters were pasted on many of the walls surrounding the square. The posters announced such quotes as: 'Smash the capitalist-roader', 'Annihilate the revisionist' and 'Destroy the reactionary authority'. Military personnel led the young people in songs, reading Mao's quotations and slogans. After waiting for hours, everyone in the square stood and raised their right arms shouting "Long live Chairman Mao." Robin recognized Mao standing at the top of Tiananmen. The scene of half a million people in a state of near riot was a chilling spectacle.

As Robin and the soldiers stood in line for the bus, he noticed that not only did everyone present a ticket but also they were required to show their personal copy of Mao's Little Red Book. The bus they boarded for their return to the compound stopped for a parade led by a drum corps and a group of shouting Red Guards. At the end of the parade, a group of victims were forced to march, likely intellectuals whose new social status was declared to be ninth-class citizen. The victims wore dunce caps and walked with their hands tied behind their backs. Most had signs hanging from their necks that stated their crimes. With Mao's endorsement, the Red Guards grew in numbers, and raided homes of suspected class enemies destroying valuable art work, antiques, and books. From the loudspeaker near Robin's compound, Red Guards recited Mao's quotations three times a day. Currently, Red Guards blasted slogans non-stop. Sometimes he heard drums and gongs passing on the street, and he knew that someone would be tortured at the former theater.

Robin asked Zhao as they walked from the bus to the hostel, "When will you have time to take me to see another movie?" Zhao replied, "There is no movie showing. The theater is now used for struggle meetings."

As many as eight Red Guard rallies frequently took place in front of Tiananmen. One rally reported over two million students participated.

Robin came to realize his small room might be the safest place for him during the Cultural Revolution. If the Red Guards were to investigate his case, they would accuse him as a rightist, traitor, foreign agent, capitalist or worse, an intellectual. He considered what torture awaited him at the hands of the militant Red Guards. It was a threat that hung over him every day. In September 1967 Robin was disappointed to read a small story in the *Liberation Army Daily* that reported another U-2 shot down by a PRC surface-to-air missile. With the Cultural Revolution occupying much of the newspaper space, a spy plane shoot down was no longer front page news. Robin believed this news indicated the U-2 operation on ROC was continuing. The prospect of his release, he realized, would not be any time soon. Inner turmoil of the Red Guards organization began to erupt, several factions declaring they were most favored by Mao himself. The country fell into chaos, and the leaders of the Red Guards were ordered to the countryside for re-education, followed a short time later by millions of rank and file.

In the spring of 1969, Mao's closest comrade, Lin Biao was elevated to the status of Mao's successor. Yang announced the news to Robin with excitement. Army personnel appeared to have been upgraded and uniforms replaced the red armbands. About the same time, armed skirmishes between the Soviet Union and the PLA along the border caused Lin Biao to issue a directive for many organizations to leave the city of Beijing believing it to be the target. People had been ordered to leave the cities to construct underground shelters for protection against possible nuclear attack.

By 1970 a few countries began to recognize the PRC, even the United Kingdom and Japan. The PRC team won the World Table Tennis Tournament Championship in April 1971, a great boost for the national pride. China invited the American team to visit, and Premier Zhou Enlai received them in the Great Hall of People. He told everyone present, "This is a new chapter in relations of the American and Chinese people."

Zhu, a new guard who had replaced Zhang, asked Robin if he could play ping-pong. He had not played since high school years, but Robin was eager for a change in his routine. Zhu led him to another room in the house where a ping-pong table sat in the middle. Without much exercise for quite some time, he enjoyed the game. Zhu said, "I will come every other day to play a game with you. You will improve your game." It was a diversion Robin looked forward to.

Some of the guards met with Robin in the afternoon, drinking tea, playing cards and table tennis. The talk eventually turned to the benefits of the Communist Party. Occasionally they took him to see a movie, but there was no excitement or anticipation of something to break the routine. His previous experience with Communist movies taught him they were very different from the ones he had enjoyed in his homeland. They were only additional opportunities to deliver yet more propaganda on the benefits of the Communist Party. The political officers preached endlessly about the merits of Communism. After one such meeting, the officers nicknamed him "Diamond Head" because they said he was so stubborn. Somehow Robin took pride in the nickname, and he felt he still had a strong grasp on his life. Robin and the officers debated Communism and Democracy much as Americans discuss the pros and cons of Republicans and Democrats, each believing his side to be the best.

Days turned into weeks and weeks to months, but still his routine in Beijing varied little. He spent a great deal of time reading and studying Mao's teachings. The political officers had not considered how difficult it would be to 'convert' Robin into a Communist. The questions in the interrogations were much the same with little variation. He complied with the orders, but Robin considered this exercise to be repetitious and boring. Zhu demanded Robin's copy of the Little Red Book. He angrily tore out the preface of the book which was written by Lin Biao. "We learned that Lin Biao is the real enemy of the country," Zhu announced, "he plotted to assassinate Chairman Mao. We are fortunate the plot failed."

After seven years in Beijing, Kuo came on a routine meeting and reported the authorities had decided he should work on a collective rice farm. He had grown up in a city and had never done farm work. However, prior experience had little to do with his future assignment. It was an opportunity to subject him to menial manual labor. Kuo announced, "Higher authority has decided you are to be transferred to a commune to learn more about the Proletarian Revolution from the peasants." Robin mildly protested, "General Liu had said when the investigation was completed, I could go back to Taiwan." Liu had apparently fallen out of favor with Communist leaders, and Kuo ordered that his name never be mentioned again. Who could Robin appeal to now? Robin asked, "How long will I be at the commune?" "Probably a year. But, you should never tell anybody that you were a U-2 spy plane pilot. It is for your own good. We will tell the officers at the commune you are a captured ROC military officer and only recently were released. Your name now is Yeh Changsheng."

'Re-education' was popular with the Communist Party during 'The Great Cultural Revolution' and many wealthy, educated citizens were targeted. Robin experienced it first-hand. He was transferred to a rural area near the City of Wuhan, two hours south of Beijing, by military plane to begin another phase of his confinement.

6

Commune Experience

A few days after Kuo's last visit, Zhu told Robin to pack all his belongings; they were going to take an afternoon train. Zhu said, "Take all that you have with you, including everything on the bed. The people in the commune are very poor, and you will not be able to buy a blanket there." His possessions were few, only basic necessities the guards had bought with some of his funds. Zhu and two other soldiers, each carrying a small bag, came in a black van to take him to the train station. He had assumed the journey might take a couple of hours, but with two additional soldiers carrying their gear, he realized that the journey might take more than a day.

Robin asked, "Where is the commune?" Zhu replied, "We are taking you to the Red Flag Commune, southwest of Wuhan." Robin knew from his navigation training, Wuhan was on the bank of the Yangtze River, more than 2,000 miles from Bejing. At the train station, Zhu directed his group to a counter designated for military personnel, where he bought their train tickets. Robin and the soldiers then followed him to the crowded platform. The military uniforms indicated authority to the throngs waiting to board the train. Zhu and his group passed through the parting crowd and boarded the train. Their assigned seats were in the middle of the coach. When they found their seats, four men already occupied them.

One of Zhu's soldiers yelled at them, "These are not your seats. Get out of here!" The four men scurried to grab their bags and find other seats. Once the train got underway, its rhythm lulled Robin into a state of fond memories riding the train in Taiwan with Betty when they were dating. Even a snippet of a memory was a chance to relive his real life. Kuo had promised he would be released after one year of re-education; he held to that promise with the same firm determination as when he was focused on his flight plan.

They had been traveling on the train for some hours when one of the soldiers needed to go to the bathroom. It was difficult to step over people and bags in the aisle. He returned a short time later and reported the toilet was also crowded with people. He would have to wait until the next station. Robin announced he would go at the next station also. Zhu cautioned, "I think you are not stupid enough to plan escaping by taking advantage of the darkness."

As he considered his situation, Robin knew that escape was not a viable option. For one thing, he had been given a little hope by the political officers that his liberation was being considered by top officials. Secondly, he had no money, no identification documents, no rations and no hope of assistance. Approved documents were required for anyone moving between towns, and citizens were required to produce authorization papers for any travel. They were interrogated about their journey's distance and destination. The distance to the eastern border of the PRC was approximately 800 miles; Robin would still have to negotiate the Taiwan Strait before being able to set foot on ROC soil. It felt a world away and would be impossible to cover on foot without great risk. This was a much different risk than he encountered flying his U-2. Although by his physical appearance Robin could blend into the local population, he did not know if anyone he talked with would report his discussion to political officers or to local police. Maybe they would identify his manner of speech as different from theirs. He had to be extremely cautious at all times. This was still an exercise in survival for him.

When the train arrived at Wuhan on the second morning, Robin's group then boarded a bus to the Red Flag Commune for another hour and a half ride. They were met at the bus station by two men, one a political officer. The other man introduced himself as Huang, a village leader of the Red Army Production Brigade. Huang was dressed in the same uniform as Robin wore. Although only a few words were exchanged, Robin had an impression that Huang was a congenial man, but he still felt he should be careful. Zhu completed some paperwork with the men. Then he gave Robin 120 Renminbi (about $18 USD), allegedly the balance of his savings from the hostel. Robin had never asked, and they had never offered to tell him the remainder of his fees which the PRC provided him. It was from these funds the soldiers had purchased necessities, such as toiletries, for him.

Administrative detail completed, Zhu and the soldiers departed. On the road to the village, Huang climbed on his bicycle and loaded Robin's pack on the back. A short time later, Huang decided to walk while Robin pushed the bicycle. The leader explained about life in the village and what Robin was expected to do there.

Chairman Mao announced The Great Leap Forward, a five-year plan spanning the period 1958 to 1963. The Communist Party's greatest legacy arguably was confiscation of land from wealthy landlords and prosperous farmers who owned large parcels of land. The party then redistributed land in rural areas among poor peasants. Each family received no more than 1.3 acres. Landowners who resisted surrendering their land were often executed. Sometimes the process of land seizure resulted in deaths of thousands of people. It was not uncommon for villagers to be executed or beaten to death by others to seize their land. By the 1950s private land ownership was completely eliminated; peasants were given usage rights to land but not full ownership. All land then was owned by the state. A typical rural family working on an agricultural commune earned the equivalent of $700 USD a year.

During the Mao era, collective and state farms produced most of the agriculture crops. (Author's note: The terms collective farm and commune were used interchangeably.) The state bought food from the farms at fixed prices, generally lower than the same products sold on the open market. With productivity low, farms were dependent on government subsidies to remain afloat. Organization and transportation problems often prevented the prompt delivery of food products to homes before it spoiled. Low productivity resulted in devastating shortages and even wide-spread famine.

Most of the agriculture sector was organized in a three-tier commune system. Over 50,000 communes dotted the country's landscape. Approximately 30,000 families relinquished ownership of all their property, tools, and animals; everything was then owned by the commune as a group. A commune consisted of 16 production brigades, each brigade composed of seven production teams. The basic level of work assignments, the production team, consisted of small village areas, from 100 to 250 people. In 1955 the Communists decreed all farmers organize into cooperatives. Party members were assigned to each commune to oversee the work and ensure decisions were made according to established doctrine. A director, responsible for day-to-day management of the commune, provided guidance to the workers. Directors additionally reported to the party cadres stationed at their cooperative to ensure complete compliance with rules and regulations.

Some collective farms were enormous; some even doubled as extremely hard labor camps for intellectuals and political prisoners. One of the largest communes, known as State Farm No. 128 of the No. 7 Division, employed 17,000 people. The farm also had some unusual features: military-style checkpoints, a foreign affairs office, television station, oil refinery and a department for marketing the crops. Dazhai Commune was one of the most famous in China. Allegedly it was re-built from ruins by 500 peasants after a flood. It served as a model for other communes. Dazhai was visited by Zhou Enlai, Deng Xiaoping, in addition to foreigners such as Queen Beatrice of The Netherlands, Pol Pot from Cambodia and leaders from Africa, Albania and East Germany. Later it was revealed that Dazhai was a sham, production figures were inflated and the commune was subsidized heavily by the government.

A big house sat at the center of the village with mud-brick and thatch houses surrounding it. The house, confiscated by the Communist Party, had been property of a landlord. Seven families now shared the big house, and Robin was assigned a room there. Huang introduced the old woman who lived in the next room. Robin greeted her respectfully, "I am going to learn from you." She looked at him, uttered a grunt and turned away. She spoke to him with authority, "Young man, you have a lot to learn." Robin learned from Huang that the old woman's husband had died in the war against the KMT and her son died in Korea in the war against the Americans. She was entitled to some privileges in the village.

Lao Taitai was a respectful title to address the woman. She taught him basic cooking skills and told him where to buy simple cooking utensils. Lao Taitai even taught him that hissing of the kettle means the water is boiled; she instructed him not to drink any water that had not been boiled. The woman even taught him to cook some vegetables like a mother instructing a child. Meat, poultry and fish were only available on certain days of the week in a store 30 minutes walking distance. Each time Robin had a chance to buy the rationed items, he shared with Lao Taitai to show his appreciation for her help.

Cloth fabric was rationed and the commune issued each person a ticket for one-foot per month. Most peasants had to save more than two years to buy a complete Mao suit. Many including Robin wore suits with many patches. Each member of the commune received an amount of grain rations, salt, oil and vegetables based on gender and age. Together, Huang and Robin went to the warehouse to set up his account for rations. That task completed, Huang gave Robin the remainder of the day to settle in.

The purpose of the party plan was to direct development of agriculture and industry. The party believed both areas had to prosper, each dependent on the other. The party provided schools and nurseries to allow adults to work. Elderly grandparents were relocated to facilities where they were cared for while all other family members worked on the commune. Robin's village consisted of 40 households, about 100 adults and half as many children of varying ages. They were responsible for the land around the village and planted three crops a year, two of rice and one of wheat or oilseed rape.

Robin lost his watch during his crash years ago, and the passage of time became difficult to determine. There was no calendar to show the current month. He only had a work schedule that planned his life for several days in the future. It was mostly an existence in which the passing of time was noted only by daylight and darkness. Thanks to the People's Republic, Robin and the other farm workers had no need for an alarm clock; they were awakened each day to a rousing musical reveille, "Red Rising Sun" as early as 5:00 a.m. Following the wake-up call, workers met in the open area, first to pay respect to Chairman Mao. They listened to announcements, reported for roll call, and participated in calisthenics. Workers then were allowed breakfast of dark bread and porridge. After breakfast, everyone filed out to their assigned work area in the fields where they toiled until dusk. The lunch break was at 12:00 p.m. and was often served near the fields. The meal was frequently a watery stew with potatoes, black bread and a little salted pork.

Robin's first impression of the farm was profound: How could a country as large as China have such extremely poor people? He observed with a heavy heart little children with no pants or shoes in the early months of winter. Would they have anything warm to wear when the weather turned colder? In this stark environment, Robin began his re-education experience. Dressed in the standard workers' black uniform, his appearance was much like several hundred other workers of the Red Flag Commune. But, he was not a typical farm worker, and he reflected sadly on how his life had changed so dramatically. He allowed himself only a brief moment of nostalgia, and returned his thoughts to his present job.

The population of his commune was divided, 12 families to a work team and 12 teams to a brigade. Each team was assigned specific tasks; some weeded the fields, some cared for the animals and cleaned the stables, some repaired tools and machinery. The Great Leap Forward moved so rapidly that by the end of 1958, 700 million people were assigned to 26,578 communes. Workers were bombarded with propaganda from every direction, even at work in the fields from the public address system. The party took pride in major construction projects completed in record time, but quality of product was lacking. However, with many of the commune residents working in the fields, there were not enough trained construction workers to build needed structures, barns, storage buildings, etc.

The Great Leap Forward also encouraged communes to build local production plants, such as furnaces which boasted 11 million tons of steel a year. Steel, coal, chemicals, timber, grain and cotton production showed huge increases in 1958 which further bolstered the party's satisfaction with the rapid progress of the five year plan. A successful harvest in 1958 was followed by a dismal one in 1959 due to floods in some parts of China. The harvest for 1959 was well below the previous year and resulted in food shortages and starvation on a massive scale. In 1960 rationing was implemented. Between 1959 and 1962 an estimated 20 million people died of starvation.

Even Chairman Mao had to admit the Great Leap Forward had resulted in failure. He resigned his position as Head of State, but remained a powerful voice as the Party Chairman. In late 1960, the Great Leap Forward was totally discontinued and private land ownership was reinstated. Communes were then reduced to a more manageable size, similar to the smaller one that Robin was assigned in 1966.

The strict organizational plan of the group farm reminded Robin of the command structure of the Air Force. He was a member of a team, the lowest level. The farm consisted of approximately 60 acres planted mostly in rice fields. The single tractor, which Robin learned to operate, plowed the fields for planting on about one-fourth of the farm; the remainder of the fields was tended with oxen. Whenever an airplane soared overhead, a rare sight, Robin paused to shade his eyes and look upward. He recalled the boy who had dreamed of flying. Would he ever feel the exhilaration of the cockpit again?

His first assignment at the farm was with the women's team; they cultivated vegetables, fed livestock and cleaned the barn. It was back-breaking work, such that he had never done in his life. At harvest of the second crop, he worked on the men's team. With no machines to harvest, everything was done by hand with hoes, harrows, and sickles, the only metal tools available. Such tools made in the local furnaces were poorly constructed and frequently the cause of workers' injuries.

The farm operated seven days a week and typically each workday was 10 hours or until the work was completed. There were no days off. If there was no need to use the tractor, he was assigned to a myriad of other mundane jobs. There was plenty of mindless, tedious work to do. Equipment and tools had to be cleaned and repaired, animals to be cared for and some areas raked or weeded. During the planting season, water buffalo helped plow the field. Maneuvering the plow and controlling the buffalo at the same time required strength and agility. Bending for hours planting the seedlings was an arduous task, and Robin felt acute back pain at the end of the workday. Workers walked the rows barefoot risking attack by leeches that hung to their legs and feet. There was little work between planting and harvest, irrigation and weeding rice fields was the only continuous labor.

Robin sometimes cooked his own evening meals over a coal stove and ate alone. The house had no heat in winter, and he had only one quilt for his simple box bed. He heated cold water for bathing from the communal pump. Credit on the farm books allowed him to purchase personal items such as toothbrush, soap and shaving items, and then worked off the credit amounts. He laundered and patched the three uniforms he was issued. The rules relaxed and conversation with other workers was permitted with the exception that he could not discuss his job before he came to the farm. The political officers told him to say only that he was 'from the other side'. Though some may have been curious, no one asked questions about his past, where he worked before the farm. The workers never questioned any authority.

Robin observed other farm workers daily, trudged about their work as they had for years, with no enthusiasm or eagerness. Their expectations were non-existent. Entire families lived there for generations, and he was the only outsider. The team leader knew about him from the political leaders who brought him, but explained his presence as someone new to work on the farm. Another pair of hands would always be welcome. None of Robin's history was offered, and the team leader was instructed not to ask about him. Major infractions of the rules by the farmers were few. Only occasionally did an exhausted worker find a hiding place for a short nap. If discovered, the team leader counseled the worker, but there were rarely any more serious punishments. The farm workers were accustomed to complete compliance without questions, and Robin's introduction went smoothly.

Prior to his capture, Robin ate most of his meals at the Taoyuan Officers Mess Hall when he was on base or he ate at home with his wife. He had little experience cooking his own meals. Now at the farm, his simple rice and vegetables at times were barely edible. Because the days were long and the work mundane, the nights were the worst. As he lay in his bed, he fought depression recalling fun times with Betty, growing up with his brothers and sisters, and, of course, flying.

"After 10 years," he wondered, "was the ROC even still working toward my release? How long will it be before I can return to my real life?" Before his capture and confinement, he had so many plans for his future: his career with the ROCAF, his life with Betty and their plans for a family. Now there was no future, only his tragic present, and it was painfully obvious that he was helpless in changing his situation.

Robin began each day as he had the previous one: Unlike the exhilaration he felt each time he climbed into the cockpit of his aircraft, he plowed the rice fields or other mind-numbing work he was assigned. All too often, he reflected fondly on his flight training. He missed the challenge of his previous job, the camaraderie of his fellow pilots, especially during his solitary meals. Now he felt this life belonged to someone else. He, too, resembled one of the farm workers who mindlessly trudged out to the fields each day.

There was only one tractor for the entire farm. He felt fortunate to be able to drive it when Huang assigned him to the task. As he drove the tractor to his work site that day, Robin returned his thoughts to the field he was required to plow. It would be better to blank out any memories of his old life. If he spent too much time reflecting how his life had changed so drastically, his work would not be completed on time. He didn't want to explain anything to the team leader at the end of the day, and he certainly didn't want to call attention to himself.

After a day in the fields, he was surprised one day to find another bed in his room. An old man introduced himself as Qin. Small and frail, Qin said he was recently released from prison. He was labeled a counter-revolutionary, one of the five black categories defined by the Cultural Revolution: Landlords, rich peasants, counter-revolutionaries, bad elements and rightists. Because of his offenses, Qin was assigned the most despicable job in the commune, collecting human and animal excrement for fertilizer of the planted fields. From Qin's conversation and appearance, Robin thought he could be about 10 years older. Qin looked very old, but prison life must have been a miserable experience that destroyed his health. Qin was a quiet, intelligent man, and Robin was content to have him as a roommate to share the cooking.

Robin often had trouble sleeping because Qin snored so loudly. When the barefoot doctor came, Robin asked for sleeping pills. The farmers who received medical training often worked barefoot throughout the rice paddies and became known as "barefoot doctors." They promoted basic hygiene, explained about preventive health care and treated common illnesses. Using Western and Chinese medicines, as well as herbs they frequently grew in their backyards, the barefoot doctors were perceived by rural farmers as peers whose advice they respected. They could also refer seriously ill people to township or county hospitals.

7

At the Center of the Storm

The meetings with the political officers resumed at the farm with Robin always asking when he could return to the ROC. On one such meeting, an officer suddenly announced, “They don’t want you back.” The impact of these words struck him with such force that he felt he had been shot down a second time and dropped from the aircraft without a parachute. He had never considered that his country would refuse to take him back. In the words of Robert “Gimo” Yang, his former squadron commander, Robin’s situation had become a political ‘hot potato’ in the ROC. With the embarrassment the government experienced at being caught spying on Mainland China, the ROC’s only response was to deny it, leaving Robin in limbo.

Robin felt betrayed and deceived. He performed the job he was trained for by his government with full knowledge of his mission. How could they deny his existence? He was enraged, resentful and saddened, but he knew his options were few. He had never felt so powerless that he had absolutely no control for his own life. Much as he was angered by the message the political officers delivered, at least he now knew that the ROC knew he was alive. Maybe his wife and his parents also knew. He now understood it was a political issue between the PRC and the ROC with him in the middle. Never had he expected to be at the center of such a problem; he had lived a quiet life always observing rules. Being the subject of a large scale dispute was confusing. The ROC was understandably trying to recover from the awkwardness of the situation while denying everything.

The meetings with the political officers ceased altogether while the Cultural Revolution raged on in Communist China. At that time, Robin experienced a little more freedom to communicate with other members of his farm team. Talking to a group of male farmers attracted little attention, but speaking with a single individual could signal more interest from the ever-present guards. Robin never knew who the snitches were, but they were most certainly present. He was always cautious about anything he said. In this environment without friends he could trust, he had to watch his back.

But at the end of the workday, there was too much time to think of what was happening to him; despair and depression overwhelmed him as his mental health deteriorated. His mother had been a practicing Buddhist when he was a boy, but Robin did not consider himself a religious person. The family did not attend his mother’s temple together. He was not yet a Christian, and he had not learned to survive on blind faith. But, he thought a lot about the past. He felt totally abandoned and considered his situation desperate. Robin acknowledged the transition from a democracy to Communist lifestyle was impossible to achieve without a feeling of extreme loss and deprivation. The forfeit of basic freedoms he had taken for granted, and the inability to exchange intelligent thoughts with his contemporaries were significant losses. He missed his wife, his parents, brothers and sisters. He hoped the ROCAF would provide solace to his wife; he thought of her every day.

A director-manager and board members composed of Communist party loyalists were responsible for the operation of each collective farm. The director controlled all the resources and incomes. At the end of each day, labor units were tallied by the brigade or team leader. Earnings were determined based on the total units entered on the books for later payment.

A short time after arriving at the commune, Huang asked Robin to lend him some money to buy cigarettes. Allegedly he had spent all his money to entertain party secretaries of the Red Flag Commune. Huang frequently asked to borrow money but never mentioned repaying it. Robin realized that Huang treated him better, assigning less strenuous jobs, and raising his work points to 10 a day. Huang assigned Robin to read the newspaper articles at the morning meetings.

It was critical that entries were accurate. When the farmers from two villages brought their produce to the warehouse, they could not agree on the accounting of their respective totals. Much depended on the accuracy of the tally. Huang, the team leader, knew Robin to be an intelligent man from the short time they worked together. The team leaders agreed that Robin had no preference for any farm group, and therefore, was perfect for the job. The solution seemed obvious: Huang re-assigned Robin to live and work in the warehouse at the farm to keep track of the production units. Most of the workers were uneducated and could not have kept their own records without help.

His room at the warehouse was much larger than at the house. A bed, desk and chair were the only furniture. An abacus sat at the center of the desktop. Robin had not used an abacus since elementary school, but with a little practice he remembered the simple rules for addition and subtraction. He tallied all the workers' points and reported the villages' totals to the satisfaction of all concerned. He observed the peasants greeting him more politely because they trusted him to maintain their accounts accurately. As the warehouse keeper, he worked only half a day in the fields. After lunch, he could rest in his room and maintain his records.

***

During his campaign for the US presidency in 1967, Richard Nixon expressed a strong interest in establishing diplomatic relations with the PRC. Soon after his election, Nixon directed his National Security Advisor, Henry Kissinger, to make subtle overtures to the PRC through other countries' diplomats in Pakistan, Paris, Warsaw and Romania. Pakistan was receptive to exchanging messages with the PRC on behalf of the US government. By opening lines of communication with China, the US anticipated the flexibility to deal with Eastern Europe. Kissinger sought to get Russia's attention without creating hostility. Nixon and Kissinger also wanted help in resolving the Vietnam War. Their goal was to put pressure on Hanoi to enter serious negotiations with the US, and to reduce the aid Russia was sending to North Vietnam. China's and Russia's agreement to engage in summit meetings with Nixon placed a higher priority on their relations with the US than with Hanoi.

The groundwork was established for Henry Kissinger to make a secret trip to Bejing. On July 9-11, 1971, Kissinger flew to Beijing from Pakistan, where he set the stage for Nixon's history-making visit to China in February 1972. For the first time in decades, American citizens observed images of China from news reports during the visit. While Nixon and his advisors engaged in discussions with Mao Tse-Tung and senior officials of the PRC, Mrs. Nixon toured schools, factories and hospitals in Beijing, Shanghai and Hangzhou with a huge contingent of the American press. Nixon announced the visit was "The week that changed the world," and indeed, substantial changes loomed in the future. Following this significant meeting, the Cold War balance shifted as the PRC and US aligned against the Soviet Union. Changes within China were taking place as a result of Nixon's and Kissinger's visits. The Chinese now recognized they could be viewed on a global stage, and they understood they needed a revised plan.

Retired USAF U-2 pilot, Robert Birkett, recalled being in Taiwan after Nixon "Played the China card." Birkett said, "I assumed part of the deal was that we would stop overflying the mainland. However, we continued flying coastal missions over international waters for another couple years, possibly to 'save face' and to let the Chinese government know that we could begin the overflights at any time if they did not keep their end of the bargain." According to Birkett, the intelligence gathered at that time could not justify the cost and the U-2s were needed elsewhere for higher priority missions. Flying missions, 15 miles from the coastline, to get the best photos after the morning clouds burned off and before the sun angle was too high, required being 'on station' from mid to late morning.

***

Following one of the mandatory evening party meetings, Huang told Robin that Kuo wanted to meet him the next day at the bus station. Robin's one year re-education in the commune was almost finished. He hoped Kuo had come to tell him he would be released to return to Taiwan soon. That night he did not sleep well, anticipating his meeting with Kuo, and hoping for the reunion with his wife and parents. After eating a bowl of rice for his breakfast, he started out walking in the early dawn though his meeting with Kuo was not until 10:00 a.m.

He arrived a couple hours early and waited at the small concession stand beside the bus station. Buses arrived and departed every half an hour. He nervously walked to each arriving bus to watch as passengers stepped out of the bus. When Kuo's bus arrived, Robin noticed he was followed by three junior officers. Kuo greeted Robin and introduced the other officers. The team was en route from Wuhan to Yueyang making this stop to visit with Robin. They would be leaving on the next bus in 30 minutes.

Robin went to the concession and ordered tea and biscuits for everyone. He noticed another star on the collar of Kuo's uniform. "You must have had a promotion, congratulations," Robin said. Kuo replied, "More responsibility, more headaches and less leisure time. How about you?" Robin explained about life in the commune, and his recent responsibility of managing the village warehouse accounting for all the produce brought there by workers. Kuo reported on the guards who knew Robin during the years he was at the hostel. Many changes were taking place since President Nixon's visit. It seemed to Robin, Kuo was just making small talk, chit chat, with nothing important. Knowing time was short, he had to ask Kuo now.

"When will I be released from the commune? I remember you said before I left Bejing that I would be released in about one year. It is almost one year now. You remember I have a wife and parents in Taiwan. I miss them very much. Please ask your superiors to consider my case." Kuo responded, "Yes, I will do that, but you have to be patient. For your information, your wife has remarried." What a devastating announcement! Robin was speechless, overwhelmed. Surely that couldn't be true. Once again, the PRC and ROC must be using him. As if in a fog, Robin could not remember much after that announcement. Kuo and his team said their goodbyes and boarded the bus. Robin stood unable to take everything in. He returned to the commune from the bus station, mindlessly walking the path, unaware of anyone else on the road. His life had never felt more hopeless than it did at this moment. Without hope of reuniting with his love, Betty, there seemed no point in looking to the future.

Robin observed that it was very easy to get pills or herbs, and he complained to the barefoot doctor of insomnia. He received two sleeping pills. Over a period of weeks, Robin met the medic with the same complaint, and received more sleeping pills. Robin secretly stockpiled the pills until he had about 100. Then one night, in desperation, he took them all at one time. If he was going to die anyway, he reasoned, he wanted to do it now rather than spend another 10 years separated from his family.

The following morning, at the time Robin read the morning news to the assembled team members, Huang noticed his absence. This was very unusual; Robin always reported to the meeting promptly. Huang sensed something was terribly wrong. He rushed to the warehouse where he found Robin unconscious on his bed, a letter to Huang, on the desk indicating he had committed suicide. Huang rushed out to call the political officer in attendance at the meeting. After a short discussion, Huang hoisted Robin on his back and walked the entire distance to the clinic, a 45 minute journey. The doctor hurriedly started medicine through an intravenous tube, and after several hours, Robin began to slowly recover.

When a nurse came to check on him, she told him Huang had carried him all the way from the village to the clinic. "You are lucky to have a village leader as strong as he is. Otherwise you would never wake up." While he recovered in the clinic, Qin, Robin's former roommate, surprised him one afternoon with a small pot of chicken noodle soup. While Robin ate, Qin told him that the news spread throughout the village very fast. By the end of the morning meeting, everyone knew of his attempted suicide. By noontime, the news came that Robin has been saved.

Qin grew thoughtful, and said, "I don't want to know what made you so desperate. Do you believe God has a plan for everybody? I always regard you as a man of clear thinking, and you must have your reason to end your life. But God has a plan for you. He led Huang to rescue you and save your life." Qin's words echoed in his head as Robin fell asleep that evening. Maybe there was something he could learn about this plan Qin said was in store for him.

Huang came the next day to check on him. Seeing he was recovering well, Huang asked Robin to follow him back to their village. Robin still felt weak, but he followed the leader. As they walked Huang said, "Did you realize if you had died, I would be in a lot of trouble? I could have been sent a long way from my family. I do not believe the reason for killing yourself as you stated in your letter. Whatever your reason, please do not do it in my village." Robin felt genuinely shameful and expressed his heartfelt apology. He had not considered that anyone would miss him if he died or that his suicide would be held against the team leader. Huang was an honorable man and did not deserve a poor mark on his leadership. He was not required to work in the fields for a few days, and remained in the warehouse. The village peasants came for their rations, but unlike their friendly greetings before his suicide attempt, they said nothing. They simply hurried away after they had collected their food.

The party secretary of the Red Army Production Brigade made an appearance after the evening meeting. He said to Robin, "You have disgraced our Red Army Production Brigade. No one has ever committed suicide. You have destroyed our good record." Other members of the commune stood and pronounced him as coward. One said vehemently, "We demand you to repent." The following day, the party secretary told Robin he was being transferred to the commune tool factory to allow him a place to start a new life. He ended the conversation,

"It is a shame your re-education has to be extended another three years." Robin simply felt nothing hearing those words. One year or three, he knew nothing would change.

In late September 1972, Robin carried his small pack and walked with Huang to the commune tool factory located outside the town near the bus station. Inside the compound was the usual large portrait of Chairman Mao facing the entrance. Huang introduced Robin to the factory leader, Zheng, and then departed to return to his village. Zheng took Robin to the living quarters where he was assigned a room with two bunk beds, a table and four stools. A rack in the room held washbasins and cups and toothbrushes. Robin put his belongings on the only bed that was not occupied, one top bunk. Zheng told Robin to begin work after lunch which was in the dining room at the opposite end of the same building.

A young man about 20 years old greeted Robin and introduced himself. "Chief Zheng told me you are taking the top level above my bunk. My name is Pan." Robin replied, "Comrade Pan, glad to meet you. My name is Yeh. You will have to teach me how to cope with life in this factory." Pan said congenially, "I am happy to show you everything here." Robin followed Pan through the dining room where they collected their food, then sat at one of the long tables. After lunch and half an hour rest, Robin followed Pan to a large building the size of a hangar filled with machines and benches of woodworking tools. They had only time for a quick look around when Zheng came to take Robin outside the building and introduced him to the blacksmith, Liang. Robin learned to pound a sledge hammer on a hot iron rod to make blanks of farm tools the commune used.

Work ended at dusk, when everyone filed again into the dining room. Robin met his other roommates, Sun and Jing. Pan told Robin that most of the bachelor workers usually played cards in the dining room after dinner if there was no evening party meeting. He asked if he knew how to play the game "Hundred Points," and Robin recalled the many times he played with his fellow pilots as they awaited flight orders in the lounge. This first evening, he felt very tired from pounding the heavy sledge hammer; so he thanked Pan and returned to his room.

After breakfast the next morning, he returned to work at 8:00 a.m. He noticed that after only two hours' work, everyone took extended breaks until Zheng rushed them back to work. No one had incentive to do much work because points were awarded based on attendance, not on production. Robin noticed that Sun and Jing changed their topic of conversation when Pan came into the room. At the evening meetings conducted by the party secretary, Robin observed Pan appeared to look for favor. He even occasionally presented himself as the deputy of the party secretary. Robin realized that Pan could be monitoring him and reporting to the secretary; he was cautious of any conversations.

Robin learned that Liang had owned this blacksmith shop, but in the 1950s it was confiscated by the Communists. Liang was sent to the poorest province in China because he refused to cooperate. The factory fell into such a state of disrepair no quality products could be made. After the PRC's admission to the United Nations in 1971, party officials finally realized technical skills were important to global recognition. Liang was recalled to the factory he once owned and given orders to repair the inoperable machinery. He was also directed to teach the workers how to operate the machines. Liang still retained pride in the factory that had been his life work for many years.

Despite the Communist Party's insistence that many of the centuries old holidays were outdated, they could not change the people's custom of celebrating Chinese New Year. Farmers took long vacations, visited relatives, wore clean clothes and played games of dominoes, a gambling game approved during the New Year holidays. Not surprising, there were rallies to praise Chairman Mao with singing and dancing in the streets. The blacksmith's shop and factory were closed a week for the holiday, and many workers traveled to other parts of the country to visit their families. Robin joined several other factory workers who walked to the nearby town to watch the celebration activities. He recalled the New Year celebrations he enjoyed with his parents, brothers and sisters many years ago: The delicious food, decorations and fireworks. He sadly recalled how his life had changed, and he wondered if they were now celebrating New Year.

8

The Curtain Opens

On October 25, 1971, the United Nations General Assembly recognized the PRC as the official representative of China. Following the PRC's admission to the UN, a number of countries sent representatives as official recognition of their relations between the countries. When PRC representatives made reciprocal visits, it became obvious the quality of life in the PRC was severely lacking and could not be improved by practice of Chairman Mao's doctrine only. Party officials began to recognize the need for technical development and education on a large scale. To that end, colleges and universities sought to open admission for factory workers, farmers and soldiers. Robin's former roommate, Pan, asked for assistance in studying for the entrance examinations.

Robin responded, "How do you know I have the capability to help you?" Pan answered quietly, "I know you were a KMT officer. I am sure you completed high school before you entered the military academy." Pan's answer was confirmation that Communist Party officials maintained a file documenting everything that Robin did and said since he was captured in 1963. Files were kept on all adults, and every activity dutifully recorded. Most significant was the fact that no one was ever allowed to see their own file to confirm or deny anything written about him or her. Robin thought the factory party secretary most likely had his file; and because Pan was a favored comrade, he would have access to the file also. This confirmed Robin's decision to be cautious in his conversations.

Robin agreed to tutor Pan in three of the five subjects: Math, chemistry and physics, subjects that Robin had excelled in at school. He recommended that Pan should study high school textbooks for the other subjects; Chinese language and politics. Successfully completing the examinations, Pan was approved for entrance at the university. He departed the commune shortly thereafter to begin his new life. Robin and his roommates had an opportunity to travel to Wuhan to visit Pan at the university. Proudly showing them around the campus, Pan pointed to his own dormitory and dining hall with much better meals than at the commune.

Browsing the area with the group, Robin spotted a used bookstore near the school. He had not seen a book or magazine in many years. Robin found a stack of old English magazines piled in a corner. Their dusty tattered condition indicated they had obviously been there a long time, and most likely no one had the intelligence to know they were English. It was a surprise they survived destruction by the Red Guards. Robin bought a few of the old magazines to read between his arc welding jobs.

In 1974, after 11 years confinement in the PRC, the original political officers returned from their own re-education experience. Robin continued to ask when he could return to the ROC. He argued that Mao's *Little Red Book* even stated people could leave, and he wanted to go. Mao's book also said the government would pay for anyone who wanted to leave. However, Robin's pleas continued to fall on deaf ears. The political officers reiterated their original response that he needed to be patient. Xu, one of the political officers, told Robin, "I have good news for you. After the New Year vacation, you should report to my office in Wuhan. You are being transferred to a factory there." Robin asked, "I can leave the commune now? I have completed the re-education?" Xu responded, "Yes. When you report to my office, I will take you to the factory."

In January 1975 Robin began another new role. The factory was actually a large maintenance yard for servicing vehicles imported from Russia or manufactured in China. He was assigned to the arc welding area of the body shop and helped other workers sanding and polishing when he was not welding. A short time later, another new experience unfolded for him. Robin learned how to repair old trucks, both military and civilian. There was actually only one model truck, called the 'Liberation', and he quickly mastered tune-ups and complete overhauls with the skills of a journeyman mechanic.

At the truck factory, he lived in a two-story dormitory with other workers and ate his meals in a community mess hall. The dormitory, like his accommodations at the farm, was unheated in winter. The truck factory operated six days a week, 10 hours a day with Sundays off. Robin received $38 a month for his work. Though it was only a little money, it was enough to buy a better meal in the village, with fish or chicken, or to buy an occasional beer with some of his co-workers. There was no entertainment or music at the restaurant or beer hall in the village. Conversation was always about inconsequential topics, never about his background. Many, he thought, knew he was from the ROC, but they never asked questions and he never offered any explanations. Often he returned to the dormitory soon after his meal in the village because there was nothing of interest to keep him longer.

Workers who lived in the city did not require a permit to travel to and from the maintenance yard by bicycle. With more leniencies at the factory, Robin decided to buy a bicycle to see the city. He was anxious to visit used book stores to buy more English books and magazines and especially a dictionary. He only had enough money to buy a used bicycle, but it allowed him a little more freedom to move around and to pursue his search without anyone observing his movements. The party secretary saw him reading one day, and asked, "What are you reading?" "An old English magazine" Robin told him. "You understand English?" he asked. Robin replied, "Not much. It has been a long time since I read any English books. I hope to refresh my memory by reading these magazines." The party secretary cautioned him to beware of Western influence such as lifestyles and capitalist thinking. Other workers were quite impressed that he read English. His roommate Sun said, "You will make big money when you are released from the commune."

Xu met with Robin monthly. He told Robin that Kuo, who was the first officer to meet with Robin after his airplane crash, had been promoted to division director of PLAAF Headquarters. Xu said, "Kuo told me to take care of you." Robin said, "I am very glad to hear Kuo had another promotion. He promised me that I would be released to Taiwan when the time was right. Has he given any news about me?" Xu told Robin, "I know you were a KMT pilot. Director Kuo told me you would be released someday. I believe you have to continue to be patient and understand he is working on your case. I am giving you my phone number if you would like to discuss anything."

On another visit with Xu, Robin said, "I know some people are receiving passports to visit relatives abroad. After 11 years, I should be permitted to go to Taiwan to visit my parents like an ordinary citizen. Please help me with this matter." Xu responded, "Director Kuo said he would like to help you, but the political climate is not clear now. We have to be very careful." At the end of 1975, more struggle and turmoil engulfed the PRC. The premier was suffering terminal cancer, and Mao's health was not any better. It was an opportunity for seizure by the Gang of Four, Mao's wife and three other zealots. Mao's wife claimed she was the only one who could understand him, and she had to speak on his behalf. No one else dared challenge her.

Mid-afternoon of September 9, 1975, workers were directed by loudspeakers to stop work and listen for important news. The party secretary of the maintenance yard then reported on the loudspeaker that Mao had passed away. Subsequently, the Gang of Four was arrested, and Mao's successor declared that his policies and directives should continue to be obeyed. Uncertainty gripped the population and no one dared say anything against Mao's teachings. Robin had no interest in either side, and he continued to read his favorite English books and magazines.

Xu came again in the spring of 1977 and announced to Robin, "I learned you are studying English." Robin replied, "Yes, I am trying to improve my English with these old magazines to pass the time." Then Xu asked, "Can you translate English into Chinese?" Robin replied, "It depends on what kind of English." Xu handed Robin some typed pages from an article in an American magazine. It reported the development of a lightweight fighter aircraft in the US. The fighter was designated as the F-16. It was the first report Robin had seen of an aircraft since his confinement in the PRC. As a military jet pilot, he had a keen interest in fighter aircraft. He was excited to know more about this one. Robin told Xu, "I would like to try. How soon do you need it?" "I am not in a hurry. Keep the article as long as you need."

The RF-101 Robin had flown could reach 1.2 Mach; the article reported the F-16 could fly twice the speed of sound. The F-16 could withstand nine G's, more than seven times that of other fighters. It had greater maneuverability in combat with the control stick on the right of the pilot's seat rather than between his knees. Another improvement was the canopy had no frame to block the pilot's view in any direction, a fascinating innovation for an aircraft. Robin quickly read the article and began the translation. He delivered the translated article to Xu only two weeks later. On Xu's next visit he brought an American Air Force dictionary for Robin to translate. Robin protested, "There are over two hundred pages. You think I can translate a dictionary?" Xu said, "You did such a great job on the translating the article. Our division said you were probably the only one who could understand the American Air Force terminology."

"But, this is a big job. I have to work at the maintenance yard in the day. I don't have a desk or any quiet time for myself in my dorm room."

"Don't worry. We can make arrangements for you."

Things moved fast when it was for the benefit of the PRC. The next week the party reassigned him to assist a technician in charge of electrical systems. He was moved to a better room with two beds, two desks and chairs, and a closet he shared with another lead man. Robin's salary increased; his first thought being he would be able to buy better meals to entertain Xu. Connections were important, and Xu was the only connection Robin had to reach the officials who decided his case. When there was no electrical work, Robin stayed in his room and worked on the translation or read other English books.

In May 1978, everyone made plans to celebrate the annual Dragon Boat Festival, one of the official holidays. The festival commemorates the death of the poet and minister Qu Yuan. A junior member of the Chu royal house, Qu served in high offices. However, when the king allied with the increasingly powerful state of Qin, Qu was banished for opposing the alliance and even accused of treason. During his exile, Qu Yuan wrote a great deal of poetry. Twenty-eight years later, Qin captured the Chu capital. In despair, Qu Yuan committed suicide by drowning himself in the Miluo River. Local admirers raced out in their boats to save him or at least retrieve his body, which is the origin of the dragon boat races. When his body could not be found, they dropped sticky rice balls into the river so that the fish would eat them instead of Qu Yuan's body.

Following the celebration, Robin's translation of the dictionary went to typesetting and final proofreading. Xu soon came with good news. "I wish to congratulate you. Your translation is quite impressive. The Party has appointed you as an English instructor in the Engineering College of Central China at Wuchang."

Robin said, "I am confused. I never thought of teaching English at a college. How could a college employ someone with my background?"

"Times are changing, and the premier instructed the party to ask professionals to solve problems. The schools are recruiting teachers and requesting organizations to recommend personnel for these positions. Our division recommended you, and you have been accepted." Robin then asked, "What should I do?" Xu told him, "Wait to receive official notice. The instructor position pays more than twice your salary now. I think we should have a big celebration."

A large meal was arranged that evening at a popular restaurant to celebrate Robin's good fortune. In addition to Xu, Robin's supervisor, the party secretary, chief of the maintenance yard, and several colleagues were invited. Robin spent a major portion of his savings for the meal, but he believed it would ensure important future connections.

With his official document appointing him as an English instructor in hand, Robin rode his bicycle to the college, the same school where he had visited Pan three years ago. He reported to Jiang, the department head who was ambivalent about the new instructor. He did not want or need another faculty member. It was unusual to have someone from the commune maintenance yard to fill a position of English instructor in college, but Jiang was not consulted for his opinion. He assumed that Robin had connections with high ranking party officials. Jiang led Robin to the faculty quarters and told him a room in a bungalow would be available for him in a week. It took several trips between the maintenance yard dormitory and the college to move his belongings. His new room had a bed, desk with chair, closet and table for a washbasin. The back door of the room led to the kitchen and latrine shared by six families also living in the bungalow. Families lived in a room the same size as the one Robin was assigned by himself. He fondly recalled what his former roommate at the commune, Qin, had told him, "God has a plan for everybody." Maybe this was part of the plan God had for him. Whatever the future held, he felt grateful for the first time in many years.

In the hierarchy of the new Communist structure, professors and teachers were considered special and merited a small measure of exceptional treatment. Robin was grateful for the elevation of his status but still somewhat uneasy that it might be tenuous. His primary duties were as a proofreader for a professor where he worked from 8:00 a.m. to 5:00 p.m. six days a week. The professor was quite congenial, and he invited Robin to have dinner with him and his family. At other times he ate his meals in the teachers' cafeteria in the company of other members of the teaching staff. Diners had a number of selections to choose from at each meal. The quality and quantity were considerably improved from his meals at the commune and maintenance yard. For the first time in many years, Robin felt a sense of being part of a community.

English was the only foreign language taught at the Engineering College of Central

China and only offered to first-year undergraduate students. The curriculum was loosely planned with little structure. They were expected to learn to read English technical publications and write simple essays in English. Jiang instructed Robin to select teaching materials from English translations of Chairman Mao's writings, party documents and periodicals. Without reference to the original Chinese documents, it was difficult to explain them correctly to the students. He was keenly aware the students had grown up with Communist doctrine, and he had to be very careful how he presented these types of materials, keeping his personal views to himself. With little time to prepare for the new semester starting in September, Robin decided to increase the English grammar portion of the course which would not conflict with political agendas.

Robin's life became extremely busy teaching 12 hours classroom instruction every week, preparing lecture notes and grading students' homework. With no typewriter available, Robin prepared lecture notes on stencil and made copies to distribute to students in class. He realized he was also learning a great deal from this experience. In the library he researched answers to students' questions to have the correct response for class. His first semester as an English instructor ended a few days before Chinese New Year 1979. After he graded his students' final examinations, he reflected on the previous months and felt satisfied that he had performed well as an instructor.

With students' favorable comments about him, word had spread about the new English instructor at the college. Many parents, who themselves had been denied education under the Cultural Revolution, pleaded with him to teach their children English. Parents were willing to spend whatever meager funds they had to provide a better life for their children. Robin had to decline politely because he simply did not have the time to spare to take on private tutoring. However, one parent who requested Robin to teach her child English could not be denied. Ouyang was the party secretary at the engineering college, and her husband was a member of the Provincial Revolution Committee. Robin was aware of the powerful positions these parents held, and the influential allies he would have. The son, Zhang Guanghua, was in high school; Robin agreed to tutor him two evenings a week at Ouyang's home.

On his day off, he spent time at the large university library that contained a surprising number of non-Communist books, such as several books on American literature among the volumes on the shelves. Robin read various European and world history books and classics such as *For Whom the Bell Tolls* by Ernest Hemingway and *Kon Tiki* by Thor Heyerdahl. Subsequently, by being promoted to Associate Professor, his salary jumped to $125 a month although his duties changed little. There was very little to spend his earnings for. He saved his money, but had no plans as for how he would ultimately use his funds.

Robin was invited to a banquet in August 1979 arranged by Yin, an instructor in the physics department, to thank those who helped him secure a scholarship to a graduate school in the US. Robin had helped Yin to fill out the application. Guests congratulated Yin on his achievement. Yin explained to the group how difficult it was to apply for a passport and the long line waiting for a visa at the American Consulate. As Robin considered Yin's comments regarding the application for passport, he thought it appeared the government had relaxed rules for travel outside China. Maybe it was time for another visit to Xu, this time with gifts of cigarettes and brandy.

Xu was surprised by the gifts, and said, "How thoughtful of you to bring gifts. What can I do for you?" Robin explained to Xu about the dinner he had attended for an instructor at his college, and what he had learned about travel permissions. "It sounds like the government has changed the policy for travel out of the country. Maybe there is a chance for me to go to Taiwan. Would you please contact Kuo and request he consider my case."

Xu explained, "Three years ago when we talked, I told you the political climate was not clear. I will explain to you exactly what I mean. When you were transferred from the commune to the factory, more than 300 KMT officers were also released from other communes and prisons. Ten generals had applied for entrance permits to Taiwan through the KMT consulate after arriving in Hong Kong. No response was ever received from Taiwan. Through intelligence sources, we learned that Chiang Kai Shek had decreed that no prisoner of war was welcome to return to Taiwan. Their cases could not even be appealed because Chiang was old and sick."

Stunned by this information, Robin had no way to know if this explanation was true. He learned Chiang had died several years earlier. The policy in Taiwan might have changed. By this time there would have been a complete change in the Taiwanese government. He kept those thoughts to himself, daring not to express anything to Xu.

9

A New Career

In 1980 the PRC government began reversing sentences of victims wrongly accused during the Cultural Revolution. One such victim was a professor at Robin's college, Dr. Qien Weichang, a PhD from Massachusetts Institute of Technology in Boston. Qien's return to China in the early 1950s was one of poor timing. The associations he made with foreigners sealed his fate. He was denounced and endured a lengthy re-education from the Cultural Revolution. In addition to his teaching, Qien continued his research in his field. He planned to publish a periodical for scholars in China to present their own research. He also wanted to distribute an English version of the journal to scholars in other countries. The English translation, completed outside the college, was so completely unacceptable as to be unusable. Qien decided there was no way he could distribute the journal to English-speaking countries. Qien requested assistance through the English department, and Robin was assigned the task. The finished product yielded the results Qien sought, only because Robin had taken the job seriously. As a result of Robin's work, Qien recommended that he be promoted to associate professor. Although it was an unusual recommendation, the party secretary, Ouyang whose son Robin had tutored, wholeheartedly concurred. In the summer of 1981, Robin was promoted again.

At a dinner for another departing university instructor, Robin learned that the honoree was leaving for Canada to visit a sister who had fled China before he was born. Even with this weak link to the west, the instructor was approved for a passport to travel. The party secretary, Ouyang, told the group that the PRC had relaxed travel restrictions because the party wanted to spread the word about progress under socialism. She added, "Travelers are encouraged to advise their relatives abroad to visit China and to invest their money here." Following the meal, Robin appealed to the secretary. "You must know my case. I would very much like to apply for a passport to go to Taiwan. My parents are getting old, and I miss them very much." She replied, "Yes, I do understand your situation. I will help you if the PLAAF approves. It may take a while."

"Thank you. I have been patient, waiting for more than eighteen years."

Three months later, Ouyang summoned Robin to her office. "Good news. The PLAAF has approved your travel to Taiwan. However, there is one problem. You are now a college professor and a valuable person to China. You can go to Taiwan, but we don't want to lose you. You have to have someone guarantee you will return after the visit."

"Secretary, you know I don't have any relatives or even good friends who would be willing to do that for me."

"Have you thought of getting married?" Robin was surprised at the question. He was approaching 50 years of age. "Who would want to marry an old man like me?"

"If you agree, the party will find a wife for you."

"Thank you." Robin thought, "If that is the only way to leave this country, I will just follow the party again." He pondered his former roommate, Qin's prophecy again that God had a plan for him. Maybe this was part of the plan.

At the end of the spring semester, a simple wedding was arranged for Ding Xiaohung and Changsheng Yeh at the English department of the university. The reception for friends and relatives was held at a nearby restaurant. The bride's brother, a few colleagues from the university and Xu joined the celebration. After a honeymoon to the Three Gorges on the Yangtze River, the couple returned to the university and Robin to his job.

After 19 years in the People's Republic of China, the political officers came in early 1982 to meet with Robin at the university. They discussed his work, and then suddenly announced, "Your request to leave the People's Republic has been granted." He was excited, but apprehensive as he thought how different things would be in his homeland after almost 20 years absence. However, the wheels of Communist China bureaucracy continued to turn at snail's pace. Regretfully, Robin had never explained his situation with the professor whose kindness he had grown to appreciate. Unfortunately, the order to leave came suddenly, and Robin was not even able to say goodbye when he departed.

By early summer, the political officers reported to Robin that he was being transported to Hong Kong to arrange for his own departure from China. In addition to his savings cache and the money he received from the PRC, he had sufficient funds to sustain himself for six months in Hong Kong. During that time he was expected to make necessary contacts to leave the country or he would be returned to Communist China. In his heart, he knew he would never again return to China, regardless of the circumstances.

In August 1982 a news article in the *People's Daily* reported two U-2 pilots, Yeh Changdi and Chang Liyi (Jack) had been approved to travel to Taiwan to visit their families. The story said the two officers had been captured in the 1960s and later appointed as civil servants in the PRC. Robin and Jack had met in Taiwan when Jack was an F-100 pilot, and Jack later transferred to the Black Cat Squadron after Robin's last flight.

The news story was quite a shock to read; Robin had not known that Jack Chang had been shot down and also captured. He could only hope for some truth to the article. Robin had been in the PRC long enough to know he could not believe this report until he was actually standing outside the border of Communist China. He could not let himself show any emotion about this news story though in his heart he wished it could be fact. When asked by his colleagues if he knew the men in the news report, Robin simply said, "I don't know them." Following an August 1982 US-PRC announcement that US arms sales to Taiwan had been reduced, the *People's Daily* reported this as a diplomatic victory. Robin now realized he most likely had been a pawn for years in a political game between the PRC and Taiwan.

Xu told Robin in early September the PLAAF wanted to offer Robin an opportunity to see first-hand some of the progress made in China before he departed for Taiwan. He could then explain this to his family and contacts in Taiwan. The plan, Xu explained, would be to travel in early October, remaining in Beijing for a few weeks. Robin was encouraged to bring his bride to join him on the tour. Xu had official business in Beijing, and he would accompany the couple on the trip. With upgraded tickets allowing them seating in a comfortable coach, the group boarded a train bound for another adventure. On October 7 they arrived in Beijing. They were met at the hotel by Wang who announced the hotel and meals were provided for the duration of their stay in Beijing. Wang also arranged transportation for them to visit the planned tour sites.

They were assigned to a two-bedroom suite with living room separating the bedrooms. Both bedrooms had private bathrooms. Robin couldn't help but compare it to his 'hotel' room provided when he was first confined in the PRC. As they were settling in, Wang reported their meals would be delivered by a soldier. He instructed them to make their own tea in the room and enjoy any program they wished to see on television. Robin marveled at the changes he observed since he was captured. In addition to the improved accommodations, there was no window in the door for outsiders to spy on his movements inside.

As he prepared to leave, Wang said, "I am always available to you. Simply call my number from the telephone here in your suite. I will see to all your needs while you are here."

Jack Chang arrived at the suite the next day. The two Black Cats shook hands and hugged, grateful to see each other. Though they did not know each other well at Taoyuan, they knew they were both shot down by surface to air missiles and captured by the PLAAF. Jack had joined the Black Cat squadron after Robin's shoot down, but the two pilots had met at the base several times.

Jack said, "I think the Communist Party had been considering releasing us since 1980 because I was appointed an instructor in the Nanjing Aviation College that year. I was assigned to teach students bench work in the laboratory. I believe they intended to show the world they had treated prisoners of war humanely."

They looked forward to many hours of talking and sharing experiences since their captures. Most certainly, both looked forward to leaving the PRC and being reunited with their families in Taiwan.

Jack said his first U-2 mission over the mainland was on October 31, 1964. He had departed from the USAF base at Takli in northern Thailand and flew by Kunming to Lanzhow and other targets on his way back to Taoyuan. After the PRC tested their first atomic bomb a short time later, the US and ROC were anxious to learn what they could about the detonation. Subsequently a few night missions were planned. The CIA realized the System 12 radar detector was not enough to protect the U-2 from surface-to-air missiles. System 13 was developed as a deceptive jammer for the enemy radar to show inaccurate readings.

On Friday January 7, 1965, Black Cat Squadron Commander Yang, told Jack the weather was improving over the target areas near Paotow nuclear plant. On Monday January 10, Jack prepared for his flight with sleep, physical exam and high protein meal of steak and eggs. Jack told Robin, "I reported to the operations office two hours before takeoff for the mission briefing. Then the technicians helped with the pressure suit. For one hour I breathed 100% oxygen." After takeoff at 6:30 p.m., Jack cruised out over the East China Sea and checked the System 13. Because of the need for radio silence, he clicked the microphone twice to signal Taoyuan that he was ready to cross the Bamboo Curtain near Shanghai. The command post at Taoyuan observed the telemetry signals were becoming weaker and then completely lost. At 9:20 p.m., the ROC Communication Intelligence Station lost Jack's U-2 position which they usually received by intercepting the PRC air defense communications. They held out hope until the fuel on board would have been exhausted. The following day, the PRC boasted in their broadcast they had shot down another U-2. On March 27, 1965 at the memorial service for all pilots who died in service that year, a monument was set for Jack at the Air Force cemetery in Taipei.

Much of Jack's capture and early confinement was similar to Robin's experience. Jack was born in Nanjing but had left home as a teenager to attend the Air Force Preparatory School. The family had fled to Chongqing ahead of the Japanese invasion in 1937. Following the Japanese surrender in 1945, Jack's family returned to Nanjing. A short time later Jack went to Taiwan with the training program. When the Bamboo Curtain fell, Jack lost all contact with his family. The interrogation officers announced to Jack that his mother and three siblings were still living in Nanjing. The PRC officers considered this relationship would prompt Jack to reveal intelligence from the ROC, but it had been 20 years since he had seen his family and there was nothing to reveal.

In 1970 the PRC told Jack that approval had been granted for him to go to Nanjing to reunite with his mother and siblings for two weeks. After the visit with his family, he was sent to a nearby commune. As with Robin's commune experience, Jack's work with the peasants was back-breaking with long hours. The workers in Jack's commune argued with the leader about the accounting of their work points. However, most of the workers were illiterate and could not have maintained their own points. The commune leader settled the dispute by assigning Jack to keep work point records, as Robin had done, a definite elevation in his standing within the group. The workers then treated him more congenially. His new assignment also allowed him time to visit his mother more frequently in her final years.

Robin and Jack had spent several hours talking about their experiences since their aircraft had crashed in the PRC. When the soldier brought their dinner that evening, Wang returned also. Wang said, "Director of the PLAAF Political Department, Kuo Di, has invited you all to have dinner with him in the Beijing Hotel tomorrow evening."

Robin said, "Beijing Hotel is where President Nixon stayed when he came to China. I was told the hotel only serves foreigners." Ignoring the comment, Wang said, "I will send a Red Flag limousine to take you there at 6:00 pm tomorrow evening." Both Robin and Jack had first met Kuo when they left the hospital following their captures. In 18 years, it appeared Kuo had made a dramatic rise in the party.

En route to the Beijing Hotel in the limousine, Robin and Jack observed drastic changes since their last visits there. The hotel was five minutes' walk from Tiananmen Square in the heart of the business district, the streets crowded with throngs of bicycles. Few people still wore the Mao suits that were required in the communes and universities where Robin and Jack had spent much of their time. When their limousine arrived at the hotel, Kuo's aide waited at the entrance to escort them to the private dining room. Kuo greeted Robin and Jack and indicated where they should be seated. With wine glass held high, Kuo toasted them. They were seated and presented so many delectable dishes, they lost count. Without doubt, it was the best meal they had since their capture. Following the last course, Kuo toasted them again. He said, "I am very happy to be able to tell you that you can leave for Taiwan now. I know you have both been looking forward to this permission for many years, but we could not treat the pilots of the world-famous U-2 spy plane lightly."

Kuo also informed them that the PRC had not received a favorable response from the ROC. Intelligence sources informed the PRC that a high-ranking official in the ROC said both pilots would be court martialed if they come back to Taiwan. Robin and Jack were shocked and confused by this recent announcement. They risked their lives in service to the ROC only to be treated like criminals. Both men were unable to even consider that no one in the free world knew they were alive so many years after their aircraft was shot down. Indeed, no one even knew they had been captured alive. The recent story in the *People's Daily* must have been a shock to the ROC government, and they did not know how to respond. Maybe they considered it more propaganda from the PRC. Robin and Jack thought this news couldn't be worse after years each spent on a commune.

Kuo added, "We are going to send you to Hong Kong. You can apply for an entrance permit in person at the Taiwan Liaison Office there. Xu will help you request a six-month visa to stay in Hong Kong. If you have not returned to Taiwan in six months, you are always welcome to return to China." Kuo was cordial and appeared to be sincere, but it was so much to take in. "The Party," Kuo said, "wants you to learn more about the progress in our country. Wang will arrange for you to participate in the Propaganda Department program to show you many of the accomplishments of our great nation. We hope you will share this information with your family and friends."

The program was scheduled to begin the following week. While they waited, Wang took Robin and Jack to a men's clothing store to have them each measured for a custom-fitted Western-style suit. He also bought them several shirts and ties, and a pair of real leather shoes, the first they had in many years. Wang told them the Party did not want them to lose face when they arrived in the fashionable international City of Hong Kong. The tour, scheduled to last two weeks, was organized by the Propaganda Department. After 18 years, both men thought two more weeks would be easy. Wang explained the agenda for the program: A lecture was scheduled for the morning, followed by a discussion and a guided tour in the afternoon. Approximately 50 people, all planning travel abroad were part of the tour; some were diplomats assuming new posts, businessmen exploring opportunities, athletes, students and some visiting relatives.

While much of the lecture could be described as more brainwashing, it was a surprise to hear that the Party admitted Mao's Great Leap Forward had been a disaster. The Cultural Revolution had caused severe damage to the country. Even with those crucial admissions, Mao was still held in high regard as evidenced by the tour of his mausoleum. Inside a room devoid of anything else was a platform holding the glass casket with the body of Mao Tse Tung. A large contingent of visitors waited to pay homage to their deceased leader. Other tours included the Forbidden City, the Great Wall, the Summer Palace, the Ming tombs, the Great Hall of People and the Museum of Chinese Revolution History, as well as sites around Beijing. They toured model facilities such as a school, factory, farm and Beijing opera. When the group visited the premier machine tool factory with 5,000 workers, Jack and Robin noted living conditions much better than when they worked in a factory.

When the program was finally finished, the Minister of the Propaganda Department hosted a dinner for all participants, with Jack and Robin seated with the host. The minister proclaimed to them that the ROC government had rejected reunification offers including direct trade, transport and mail. When he asked for their opinions, both men had no comments. It was not surprising at the end of the meal when the minister told the group, "Don't forget you are representing your motherland. You have the responsibility to spread the word of our government policy." It was just once more opportunity to spread a bit more propaganda. Xu reported to Jack and Robin that he had received the Hong Kong visas for them, and they were now approved to travel. However, the Minister of the Education Department and the Minister of the United Front Department wanted to host farewell dinners for them, but both ministers were very busy now. With no other choice, Jack and Robin continued to wait.

At the dinner with the Minister of the United Front Department, the 'one country, two systems' policy touted by the PRC was again a subject of conversation. Robin then realized their release from the mainland to reunite with their families was secondary to the PRC's agenda for them to carry out the Communist government's policy. Both men sat and listened politely with no comments to offer.

In early November, Xu accompanied Jack and Robin on a flight from Beijing to Guangzhou. They stayed the night in a hotel, and the next day boarded a train to Shenzhen, the border town across from Hong Kong. On November 10, 1982, 19 years and nine days after his shoot down, Robin arrived at the border station. Though he had waited for this day for years, he was now apprehensive about the forthcoming process. A short walk from the train depot, the bridge spanned the Shenzhen River between the mainland and the British Crown Colony of Hong Kong. A small wood structure on the Chinese side of the river served as the gatehouse. A line of people waited to enter the building.

Xu told Robin and Jack he could not go into the gatehouse with them but explained what they could expect. Once inside officials would check their travel documents. When they were given authorization, they would be allowed to cross the bridge to Hong Kong. On the other side of the river, Hong Kong police would also check their documents. Xu told them, "A travel agent named Pei from China Travel Agency will meet you. He will take care of all your needs in Hong Kong." Xu then shook hands with both men, wished them good luck and turned to walk back to the train station.

While waiting in the line of people entering Hong Kong, Robin heard some speaking Taiwanese. Robin asked one man if he had a nice trip to the mainland. The man responded he had visited his grandparents whom he had never met before. Robin asked, "Where do you travel next?" The man answered, "Back to my home in Taiwan." "Then why do you go to Hong Kong?" The man explained to Robin that the ROC would not issue a passport if they knew he was going to visit the mainland. The mainland government does not accept the ROC passport either. The traveler explained they had to apply for entrance permit to the PRC Consulate in Hong Kong. When he returned, he had to go through the reverse process.

Jack and Robin finally made it to the front of the line, and their documents and bags were inspected. Both were given approval to pass through the gate to the bridge. Only a few steps forward, but a major life change. On the bridge, both men paused to breathe a huge sigh of relief – freedom at last. They continued on to the Hong Kong side where the British flag flew proudly in the sun. Robin had lived in Hong Kong with his family when he was a young boy, but it was now almost unknown to him. He was unsure of his future, but at least he was free again. From now on he could make his own decisions.

10

Hope

As Xu had told them, Pei, the travel agent, waited outside the customs office and escorted them to another train en route to their hotel, The International, a reservation made by the PRC government. They checked in at the hotel front desk and Pei showed them to their room. Pei said, "My travel agency will pay your hotel bill. I am also authorized to provide you with funds for living expenses for the first month in Hong Kong." He gave Jack and Robin $2,400 Hong Kong dollars each, equal to approximately $12 US dollars per day. As he prepared to leave, Pei gave them his address and phone number and told them to call at any time if they needed help. Jack asked quickly, "Do you know where we can find the Taiwan Liaison Office?" There was no Taiwanese Embassy or Consulate because the country was not recognized by the PRC. "I don't know the exact location, but I will find it and call you."

When Pei departed, they observed the room more closely. Two beds were topped with thread-bare blankets and flat pillows. A few bent rusty wire hangers dangled on a metal rod for their clothes. Cigarette burns dotted the top of the four-drawer chest. A small scarred table and two battered mismatched straight chairs completed the décor. Other travelers they saw in the hotel appeared to be from mainland China; all spoke Mandarin, not English or Quangdong dialect. Jack and Robin suspected the travel agency and the hotel were PRC owned. Once again, they believed someone could be listening to their conversations. They would continue to be cautious. When in Hong Kong, Robin's and Jack's pictures appeared in the *People's Daily* newspaper, a publication circulated worldwide. It was common practice for Communist China to announce the release of prisoners because they believed it made their government appear charitable to the outside world. The short story that accompanied the photos did not mention any details.

Pei called to tell them the address of the Taiwan Liaison Office where they could apply for entrance permits. "Two photos," he said, "will be needed for each application." Jack and Robin dressed in their new suits, though ill-fitting, and set out for the liaison office as their first order of business in Hong Kong. They filled out the applications and provided the photos Pei had told them to bring. The clerk took the forms and told them to return in one week for their permits. Both men were buoyed in spirit believing there would be no problem returning to Taiwan, and they looked forward to returning in a week. They could then make plans for airline travel.

Time passed slowly before they could return to the liaison office. They decided to shop for some more contemporary clothes so they wouldn't stand out in their poorly-tailored suits. The day finally arrived and Jack and Robin eagerly traveled again to the liaison office to claim their entrance permits. They gave their names to the clerk who said, "Please wait here." She left them to go to another office and returned with a man who was not even courteous enough to introduce himself. The man simply said, "We are very sorry, but your applications have been rejected by our government." Jack and Robin both asked, "Why?"

"I do not know why. We were only advised the applications were rejected. We are very sorry." The man quickly turned and left, leaving Robin and Jack stunned.

They were both accustomed to disappointment throughout the last 18 years and this was certainly one more unexpected setback. There was more than one way to let the Taiwanese government know they wanted to return. The current president was Chiang Ching Kuo, son of Chiang Kai Shek. The president had been to the Black Cat Squadron many times as the Administrator of the ROC U-2 Project. He had met each of the pilots. Surely the president would know the risks the pilots had taken to complete their missions. Maybe they could find a way to reach him.

On the way back to their hotel, Jack thought he recognized a former Air Force Preparatory School classmate, Li Chingyueh, waiting with a China Airlines crew in front of the Imperial Hotel. Li and Jack had been assigned to the same ROC F-84 fighter squadron for several years before they were assigned to the Black Cat Squadron. Jack stopped the man and asked, "Are you Li Chingyueh?" Li was stunned, "Chang Liyi? I can't believe it is you. We knew you were shot down over the mainland." Jack replied, "Yes, I am Chang Liyi. It is a long story. Do you have time to talk?"

Li said, "We are on the way to the airport for our next flight. Another of our classmates, Liu Jetchuang, will be coming to Hong Kong in a few days. He is a captain at Far East Airlines. I will tell him to get in touch with you."

When Liu called a few days later and offered to come to The International, Jack said it would be better if he and Robin came to the Imperial Hotel to meet him. The three former U-2 pilots had dinner together and talked for hours of their experiences in the Black Cat squadron. Liu said, "I completed U-2 training in Tucson, Arizona and returned to Taiwan to join the Black Cat Squadron. When I returned in 1965, you both had been reported lost over the mainland. I completed 10 overflight missions, and then was released from U-2 duty. I later became the Black Cat Squadron Commander from 1970 to 1972. The squadron was disbanded in 1974. I retired then from the ROCAF and became a captain with Far East Airlines." Jack was anxious for word about his wife. He asked Liu, "Do you know my wife, Chaichi?"

"I think she works for China Airlines now. Shichu (Gimo) Yang is now a captain at China Airlines, and I'm sure he would know her. I will ask him to see you when he comes here again in about two weeks." Yang was deputy commander of the Black Cat Squadron when Robin was there. He was subsequently promoted to squadron commander when Jack flew in the group.

Liu discussed the options with Robin and Jack to make contact with President Chiang. They drafted a letter to General Julin, Commander in Chief of the ROCAF, expecting that he would deliver it to the president. Liu offered to deliver the letter when he returned to Taiwan. Before they departed for the evening, Liu offered the most comforting words Jack and Robin had heard in many years. "China Airlines and Far East Airlines have contracts with The Imperial Hotel and all our crews stay here when they layover in Hong Kong. Many of the pilots were our classmates. If you need any help, you can find someone here. They will all do what they can for you."

The next week Gimo Yang arrived in Hong Kong, having flown overnight to meet the two released aviators. Jack and Robin walked the short distance to The Imperial Hotel. It was an emotional reunion for the three former Black Cats. Gimo, who had also seen their photos in the newspaper, believed the location of their hotel was no coincidence. Their hotel had been arranged by the PRC to be close to the Imperial where China Airlines crews stayed. Gimo was retired from the ROCAF and now a senior pilot for China Airlines. He told Jack that his wife had already contacted Gimo and asked how she could help with the men's return. She also worked at China Airlines, and saw Gimo frequently in the course of their respective flights.

Gimo said, "I know your letter was delivered to General Julin; I requested an appointment with him to discuss your cases. Julin and I were in the same fighter squadron when we were both young pilots. The bad news is that he has refused to see me."

Gimo urged Jack and Robin to be patient; they had many friends and classmates who were willing to help them. As the men continued to talk, Gimo told each of them what he knew of their families. He told Jack about his children who were now in graduate school, college and high school. Gimo said he expected Jack's wife to be in Hong Kong in about 10 days, and she planned to tell him in more detail about their lives. Jack was anxious to see her, but he understood a lot of time has passed. Maybe she did not feel the same about him. He told Robin his parents were still living in Taiwan and his brother, Warren, had immigrated to the US after retiring from the ROCAF. Gimo said, "Warren and I were close classmates. I apologize," he added delicately, "but I have lost contact with your wife, Betty." Robin said, "One of the PLAAF officers told me quite some time ago that she had remarried."

Gimo responded, "I heard that too, but I didn't want to tell you."

They had been in Hong Kong one month, and the travel agent, Pei, came to deliver their per diem for the next month. They talked briefly, and Pei asked, "How is it going with your applications for entrance permits to Taiwan?" Robin said, "They have rejected our applications with no explanation. We are working to make contact through other channels."

Pei said, "If you need help, I have a friend who works for the Hong Kong branch of the New China News Agency. If you are interested, I could ask him to publish some articles in the newspaper to put some pressure on the ROC government." Jack and Robin thanked Pei. Jack said, "We think it may be too early for that, but we will keep it in mind." They knew they should be careful about considering Pei's offer. They could be used by the PRC government to send a conflicting message. Experience told them the PRC government would still be keeping tabs on them.

Robin received a letter at the hotel from Betty's sister, Helen Tsai, who had seen his picture in the newspaper and immediately called Betty. The sisters planned a trip for Helen to come to Hong Kong with money for him from his family en route to visit the sisters' parents in Taiwan. Even Betty had sent money, and a package containing a letter and mementos of their time together. Everyone was eager for news when he would be coming home. Helen also delivered sad news and confirmed to Robin that Betty, believing him to be dead, had remarried in 1969. She lived in Princeton, New Jersey, with her husband and two children. Although Robin was disappointed and saddened by the news, he could feel no bitterness. She was as much a victim as he had been.

Robin called his brother, Warren, who lived in Las Vegas, Nevada. His brother was excited to announce to the family that Robin was alive in Hong Kong. It was uncertain how Robin would leave Hong Kong or even where he would go from there. Eager to do what they could to help, his brothers and sisters quickly collected a sum of money for him. A few days before the Chinese New Year, Gimo called Robin and Jack and asked them to come to his hotel. They told Gimo they had heard nothing promising from any of the friends who traveled to Hong Kong.

Gimo announced, "I finally have an answer from the ROC government. You will be treated according to a new regulation that states: 'All military personnel captured by the Communists must stay in a third country for more than five years before applying for an entrance permit.'"

Jack said, "But our permits only allow us to stay in Hong Kong for six months. How can we go to another country for five years?"

Eagerly Gimo explained, "Do you remember Russ, the American U-2 pilot in the Black Cat Squadron? Russ was an alias; his real name is Bob Erickson. He is now retired from the CIA and lives in California. We have maintained our friendship since we both retired from our agencies. I called him to ask if he could contact some people at the CIA to ask for help. He said he would be willing to do what he could, but he needed a letter from each of you explaining your present situation and expressing your interest in staying in the US." Robin and Jack eagerly agreed to write their letters for Gimo to send to Erickson.

Gimo warned, "I believe contact with the CIA will be a longshot. The Black Cat Squadron was terminated years before. Even when the program was active, interaction with the CIA was always considered confidential. It might be unlikely that anyone at the Agency would agree to help now."

11

Freedom

A month later Gimo returned to Hong Kong and reported news about his trip to deliver their letters to Bob Erickson. Bob had contacted the former director of the CIA U-2 project, General Jim Cunningham. Although Jim was also retired, he still had influential contacts in the Agency. Jim told Bob, "Those men have done so much for our country. Let them know we will take care of them." Bob told Gimo to return to Hong Kong and take Robin and Jack to an office where they would meet a US official named Charlie. Following an interview, Charlie told them the US was willing to help them. Fearing a delicate political situation if the PRC knew the US was providing help, Charlie recommended they both immediately cease communication with everyone affiliated with the PRC, including the travel agency and the hotel staff.

Charlie said, "The Royal Hong Kong Yacht Club is a good place to stay, and we recommend you move there immediately."

Before they left the office, Charlie gave each of them $3,000 for which they were asked to sign a receipt. Charlie also gave each of them his telephone number. Both Robin and Jack were reminded of the contrast between the ROC's denial of their entry permits and the willingness of the US to help them. To avoid any appearance of departure from the International Hotel, both Robin and Jack walked out of the hotel the next morning with their papers stuffed securely within their layers of clothing. Everything else was left behind in the hotel, and there were no checkout documents. Robin moved to the yacht club, as Charlie recommended and Jack stayed with a friend on Hong Kong Island. Fearful of being observed by PRC agents, Robin spent most of the time in his room watching television or reading newspapers.

After a month of no response from Charlie, Robin called him to report the expiration date of his Hong Kong visa was close. Charlie reported that the US was negotiating with the ROC for passports for him and Jack. Once passports were issued, the US would then approve visas for their authorized entry into the country. Robin was getting very nervous about the approaching expiration date. If the US was unable to help, then he would be an illegal resident in Hong Kong, subject to deportation back to mainland China. It was the last thing he wanted to contemplate.

With just one day before their visas expired, Charlie came to tell Robin and Jack they could leave the following day via Pan American Airlines on a flight to the US. Charlie accompanied them to the airport via ferry and taxi. The three men went to the Pan American counter where Charlie left them while he met with officials in the back office. He returned with tickets and boarding passes, and told them when the flight landed in Los Angeles, they would be met by a gentleman who would help them with the remainder of the process.

The flight from Hong Kong to Los Angeles had a stopover in Tokyo, but Robin and Jack were not allowed to leave the Pan Am area of the terminal. They were both still apprehensive about the next leg of the flight. While they waited for the flight to Los Angeles to be called, they felt their lives now moving rapidly. Their fear of the PRC reach for control was so

Robin, John Raines and Jack Chang after arrival in Los Angeles. (Robin Yeh's collection)

profound; they believed they would still be removed from the flight and returned to China. Worse yet, if they made it on the plane, they feared the flight would be hijacked to prevent them from reaching the West. It was a long 12-hour flight, allowing too much time to reflect on the past, missions completed, airplanes flown, and families left behind. Robin and Jack were again nervous about arrival in Los Angeles. They knew they were being met by someone, but they knew nothing of the plans beyond that.

Their airplane touched down at Los Angeles International Airport and taxied to the gate. As their aircraft door opened, they waited. A tall man wearing a Black Cat jacket and cap came forward and said, "*Nǐ zěnmeliǎo jiāng mattr? Nándào nǐ bù jìdé yǒu péngyǒu ma?*" ("What's the matter? Don't you recognize an old friend?"). They suddenly recognized this former friend and coworker; they rushed to him for a huge welcome greeting. John Raines had met Robin and Jack at Taoyuan Air Base where he was a CIA special agent assigned to Detachment H. He had frequent contact with the Black Cat pilots at the squadron and off duty at the Officers' Club. John ushered them through a special immigration area processing, and then accompanied them to their next Pan Am Flight to Washington, DC. As they boarded their flight, John told them there would be another agent to meet them when they arrived in Washington.

The aircraft touched down at Dulles Airport in the late afternoon. Robin and Jack were once again nervous about what lay ahead. Whatever it might be, they knew now they

Robin and John Raines at 2002 reunion. (Robin Yeh's collection)

were free men. They were met at the gate by General Jim Cunningham, the Agency contact who facilitated their return. General Cunningham said, "I wanted to meet you personally, and welcome you both to the US." It was also chance for Robin and Jack to express their appreciation for his help in getting them out of Hong Kong. Cunningham brought another agent, Frank, who would be responsible for helping them become acquainted with all things American. Frank took them to their new two-bedroom apartment courtesy of the US government, including their living expenses. "This arrangement will continue," Frank explained, "until your immigration status is settled."

Robin and Jack recognized the contrast between the help they were receiving from the US, which realistically had no responsibility for them, and the ROC. They were advised that a ROC Air Force officer was expected to arrive in Washington soon to discuss the ROC's position regarding their status. The ROC had not considered the resourcefulness of the former airmen and their friends and colleagues. Two weeks later, Major General Lin Hsiche, Deputy Chief of Staff for Intelligence, ROCAF, came to Washington DC. He met with US officials and Robin and Jack.

General Hsiche said, "The ROC does not encourage military personnel to surrender instead of sacrificing their lives for their country." Neither Robin nor Jack had received instructions prior to their flights indicating that policy. That they had survived a horrific aircraft crash was somewhat of a wonder. It added insult to real injury to even suggest they were expected to take their own lives.

There was some discussion that Robin and Jack had been directed to take their own lives rather than allow their capture. However, a review of the preflight briefing tape recording indicated there was no such directive. Both pilots confirmed they had not been given that order. They were not issued any type of weapon nor lethal medication. They were told in the briefing, if captured, "You are to say you are a pilot of the 6th Group on a routine patrol." General Hsiche said, "I have negotiated with the US officials to grant you permanent resident status. The US will provide pensions to each of you for the rest of your lives. The ROC will give you $100,000 USD as back pay and pension." The general further explained that President Chiang Ching Kuo was in poor health and Wang Sheng had been designated to act on his behalf. General Hsiche said should this matter go through Wang Sheng, he would be expected to deny their appeals.

Days later, the Agency contact, Frank, returned to their apartment. He told them the US government had granted them political asylum and would help them obtain an immigration visa, commonly known as a 'green card'. He explained they would then be permitted to work with the green card. Until the time that they were self-sufficient, the US would continue to provide their living expenses. Frank said, "We ask that you not let the PRC government know your situation, and do not communicate with anyone in the PRC. However, you are free to communicate or visit with friends or relatives in the continental US or to communicate with anyone in Taiwan." To further assist Robin and Jack in becoming familiar with the American way of life, Frank sent a Chinese-speaking coworker to meet with them. Mr. Chen helped them apply for Social Security numbers and driver's licenses. He took them to a grocery store and shopping mall, and Chen even drove them sightseeing around Washington, DC on weekends.

Three months later, Frank reported to them that the CIA and ROC has reached an agreement for the provisions of their support in the US. The CIA would provide them $200,000 each and the ROC would pay them $75,000 each. The funds were to be invested for them and the interest paid every six months. Until they received their first interest payment, Robin and Jack were given $25,000 each. Jack's first journey was to meet his daughter in Dallas, Texas, who was only seven years old when he was captured in the PRC. It was a somewhat awkward visit because neither knew much of the other, but they appreciated the time to get reacquainted. Robin flew to his brother, Warren's home in Las Vegas, for a family reunion of his siblings. The visit was a busy one, each eager to learn about Robin's experience. They all told him about life in the US and the opportunities he would have. Mostly, they were all happy to know he was safe now.

Robin's and Jack's green cards arrived in October 1984, granting them the opportunity to find jobs to support themselves. After being in the Washington, DC area for a year, Robin decided he wanted to settle in a warmer climate. Helen, his former sister-in-law, told him she and her husband were investing in a restaurant in Houston, and they invited him to be the manager. Restaurant operation had not been his first consideration, but he had few choices at this moment. He eagerly accepted, and prepared for a move south to Houston.

Robin had one more thing to do before closing that chapter of his life. With considerable apprehension, he met with Betty in Princeton, New Jersey, for what he recognized would be the last time. It was a sad and poignant meeting, each understanding that fate had devastated their lives and robbed them of a future together. Through tears of anguish, Betty said over and over, "If I had only known." However, Robin was realistic, and he believed it was appropriate for Betty to resume her life. Without bitterness, he wished her much happiness and prepared to resume his own life.

Robin's aging parents, still living in the ROC when he was released from the PRC, were excited to learn of his survival. His mother had always refused to believe that he was

Keiko and Robin at their home for a birthday celebration. (Robin Yeh's collection)

dead. They talked by phone and were happy to know he was now safe. Because he was not permitted to enter the ROC, even for a brief humanitarian visit, Robin was unable to see his father, Wei-Sheng, before he passed away. His mother, Shi-Wueng Shu, later moved to California to be nearer her sons and daughters who had immigrated to the US. Robin was able to spend a great deal of time with her in her last years, and they both cherished that time together.

By 1990, the political climate in ROC had changed and members of the senate discussed Robin's and Jack's treatment by the previous government. In an attempt to make amends, the government invited them to return to the ROC for 30 days, all expenses paid including first-class air travel. By this time Robin planned to marry Keiko Tu, a lady he had met through a mutual friend in Houston. When the ROC officials learned of his impending wedding, they encouraged him to bring Keiko and they provided all the details for the ceremony and reception. Robin was interviewed by television and newspapers and treated to a hero's return, some 28 years after he departed on his fateful flight. The current ROC government did the best it could to provide reparation for the misdeeds of the previous administration. Robin felt honored to be recognized for the years he spent in the PRC as a result of his honorable service to his country.

With the excitement and thrill of aviation still in his heart, he studied for and received a private pilot license. He soon realized, however, that the small, slow airplanes were like playing with toys after the fighters he flew in the ROCAF. Robin compared flying the small airplanes to driving a Volkswagen after speeding around in a Porsche. He decided not to renew his license, and his wife, Keiko, was happy with that decision. She found it difficult to be supportive knowing what he had endured because of another airplane.

In 2005 the 4080th SRW honored the Black Cats at the reunion in Del Rio, Texas, where some of them had trained. Nine Black Cats and their spouses were in attendance:

Robin Yeh, Jack Chang, Mike Hua, Chris I, Robert (Gimo) Yang, Andy Fan, Mory Tsai, Johnny Shen and Joe Wei. The Taiwanese pilots came from across the US, Taiwan and Canada to attend the event. General Mike Hua spoke to those present on behalf of the Black Cats. They toured Laughlin AFB which appeared quite difference than in the 1960s when they trained at the base. During the three-day event, the old friends and pilots enjoyed the camaraderie with their USAF colleagues.

On October 8, 2011, the Armed Forces Museum in Taipei, opened a special exhibit titled, The Brave in the Upper Air, honoring the Black Cat Squadron. The President of Taiwan and the Minister of Defense attended the event. The president opened the exhibit with a welcome address to the honorees and guests, and recognized the contributions of the unit. They were treated to a tour of Taoyan where their squadron had operated. Following the tour, the group attended a special dinner in their honor.

Robin and Keiko resided in Houston where he was active in the Chinese Community

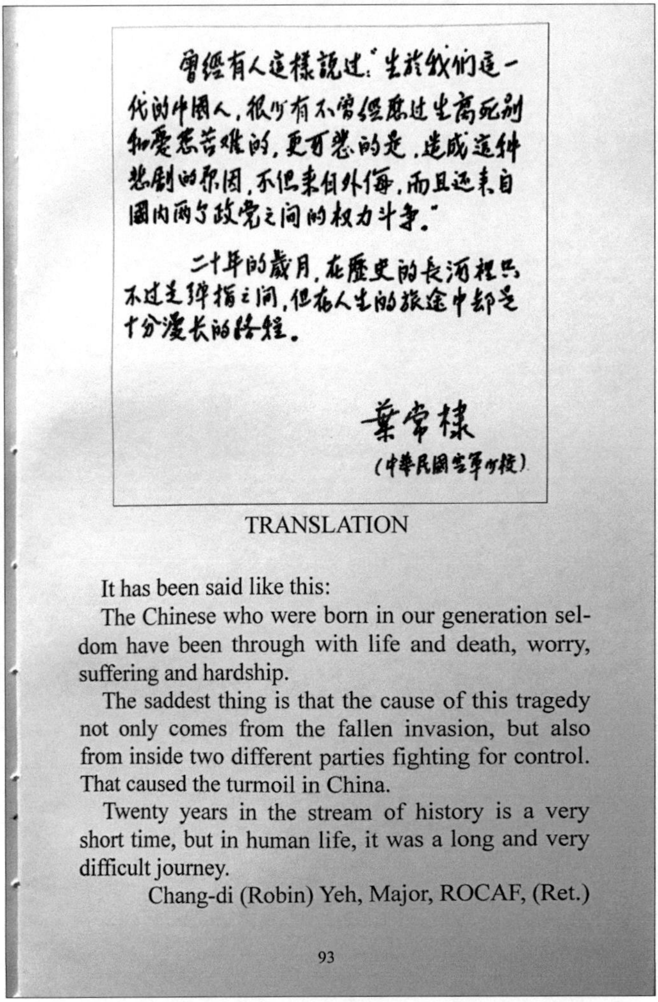

曾經有人這樣說过："生於我们這一代的中國人，很少有不曾經歷过生离死别和憂患苦难的，更可悲的是，造成這种悲剧的原因，不但来自外侮，而且还来自國内两个政党之间的权力斗争。"

二十年的歲月，在歷史的長河裡只不过是弹指之间，但在人生的旅途中卻是十分漫长的路程。

葉常棣
(中華民國空軍少校)

TRANSLATION

It has been said like this:

The Chinese who were born in our generation seldom have been through with life and death, worry, suffering and hardship.

The saddest thing is that the cause of this tragedy not only comes from the fallen invasion, but also from inside two different parties fighting for control. That caused the turmoil in China.

Twenty years in the stream of history is a very short time, but in human life, it was a long and very difficult journey.

Chang-di (Robin) Yeh, Major, ROCAF, (Ret.)

93

A statement written by Robin. (Robin Yeh's collection)

Center activities. He volunteered at Second Blessing Community Church resale shop and he exercised several times a week at a nearby fitness center. Together, they attend regular Sunday and weekly Bible study classes at the Southwest Lutheran Church. Since his school days in Shanghai, Robin had been an avid soccer fan; he watched it on television as a captivated spectator regardless of the teams playing.

Robin attended bi-annual U-2 pilots' reunions as a member of the Dragon Lady Association and enjoyed the camaraderie of his fellow pilots, both USAF and ROCAF. After having lost 20 years, Robin enjoyed each day of freedom as a gift and focused on leading a full life in the company of friends and family.

12

Final Flight

Robin, Keiko and I had lunch on Monday October 3, 2016 just six days prior to their move back to Taiwan. We ate at a favorite restaurant near Houston's Chinatown. That day we talked mostly about their forthcoming move, selling their home and car, packing and mailing some big boxes before they departed. The delivery of the boxes would take about a month, but they already had sufficient clothes and personal items at the apartment in Teipei that had been Keiko's mother's home prior to her death. Conversation turned to travel and they asked me if I would come to Teipei. It has always been on my bucket list to visit the Taiwan and I hoped with friends there I would have a big reason to go. Lingering over our tea and we recalled some of the events and memories we shared: 4080th SRW reunions, having lunch together about every six weeks, the Black Cat friends and meeting to celebrate our birthdays. It was finally time to release our table at the restaurant and reluctantly say our goodbyes, each of us unsure when the next time we would meet.

As I drove out of the parking lot of the restaurant, I looked in my mirror and saw Robin and Keiko still waving at my departing car. I felt a big wave of sadness on my drive home. On Robin's birthday, November 1, 2016 I emailed him to wish him a happy day. His reply to me was the last I would receive.

On November 17, 2016 Xu Lin, emailed to ask if I was aware that Robin had a heart attack and passed away two days prior. I was absolutely stunned and saddened. However, on reflection, I was happy that Robin had returned to his homeland where his father is buried. I texted my journalist friend in Teipei, Tang Yi-Ning, who I had met through Robin some years before. She and I have maintained contact thanks to Facebook and email. Yi-Ning told me that she had planned to attend Robin's funeral which the Air Force was arranging and she promised to send me photos. When I received the photos, I was surprised but grateful, to see that Robin had finally received the hero's tribute he deserved from Taiwan. He would have been humbled to know that the current President of Taiwan, Tsai Ing-wen and the past president, Ma Ying-jeou, were among the many mourners.

In the years that I had known Robin, I was amazed that he had long ago released whatever anger and resentment he had toward his country. I found him to be a gentle man, kind, quiet and thoughtful. Sometimes we never know what influence people we pass in life may have on our own destiny. I choose to believe that Qin, the old man Robin met while he was at the farm in Mainland China, was a wise man. It was he who planted the seed for Robin that God had a plan for him. Robin found Christianity through his wife, Keiko, and they attended church together in Houston.

I will miss my friend, but I am comforted to know that he will be flying in God's home now.

Linda Rios Bromley

Keiko, Robin and me at our last lunch. (Author's own collection)

Displaying Republic of China flag. (Tang Yi-Ning)

Presenting Robin's widow, Keiko, with a flag. (Tang Yi-Ning)

Honor Guard. (Tang Yi-Ning)

Memorial procession. (Tang Yi-Ning)

Memorial procession followed by Robin's widow, Keiko, and dignitaries. (Tang Yi-Ning)

Display honoring Robin Yeh. (Tang Yi-Ning)

Robin's Black Cat cap. (Tang Yi-Ning)

Appendix I

Remembrance of Members of the USAF and Friends

From Charles W. Kern
We had frequent interactions with the ROCAF pilots, inviting them to our home for steak or burger cookouts and drinks. They enjoyed playing with our two sons, Wes and Will, who were seven and eight years old. Our sons really liked being with the Taiwanese pilots; it provided them a different view of life outside the US.

While I was occupied with the charcoal grill and the burgers or steaks, my wife, Nancy, sat in on some of the games. Our family enjoyed hosting these gatherings at our home on base. The Black Cats were a great bunch of guys and our feelings of camaraderie and respect went both ways. It was with great sorrow when we learned of one of them being shot down, killed or captured.

A few years later when I was doing temporary duty assignment (TDY) at Bien Hoa, Vietnam, I was sent to Taipei to pick up a load of brass cannon shells that had been converted into 'Trophy Mugs'. Several of the Black Cats met me and paid me back for the good times they experienced in the US. We all had a superfine evening together, dining and boozing. We had quite a few toasts, *Gam Bai*?

From Will Kern, Son of Charles W. Kern
Taiwanese pilots, Billy, Bing and Johnny, came to our home when we lived on Cass Avenue on Laughlin AFB. They were all very nice and cordial. Johnny was particularly kid-friendly, probably because he had kids who he missed while he was taking pilot training in the US. I remember all of them as young men, short, dark hair, and chestnut-colored skin with taut muscles. Well-built as I recall. They dressed casually with polo-style shirts. Once they made fried bananas for us which we thoroughly enjoyed.

From Wes Kern, Son of Charles W. Kern
My brother, Will, and I had just come home from the movies where we saw some old cartoons showing buck-toothed Japanese getting their butts kicked by Popeye. When we came into the house and saw several Asian men, one of us (probably me) yelled "Japs!" In our young minds, Japanese and Chinese were all the same. Within a split second, my dad yanked both us into the bedroom and read us the riot act. He explained these men were guests in our home and were to be treated with respect. That resolved we made fast friends with Billy, Bing, Andy and Johnny. Not only did they make us fried bananas, but they also built kites for us. We all then went out to the prairie behind our house and launched the kites.

From Anthony Martinez
The first group of trainees for the Carbon Copy Project we had in the 4080th SRW was in the RB-57D, 4025th RS, 1957 or 1958. Colonel Yang led the first group of Taiwanese

trainees for the Carbon Copy Project at Laughlin. A few years later, when the 4080th SRW moved to Davis Monthan AFB, Arizona we had another group of Carbon Copy trainees in the U-2, again led by Col Yang. They were all fine of young pilots, very cooperative and eager to learn. One of our navigators, "Muddy" Waters, and his wife entertained them and helped make them feel comfortable in a very foreign environment. Many of our USAF pilots invited them to our homes for weekend barbeque, and we found them to be congenial gentlemen. Their training with us lasted about two months. After they returned to Taiwan, I believe that they were committed to fly at least 20 overflights of mainland China before they returned to their regular unit. Several were shot down over China by SA2 missiles as they flew extremely long missions from Taiwan to Lop Nor on the far western part of the mainland where the missile test site was located. They flew a long and straight flight line as it was stretching the range of the fuel supply of the aircraft. Some were shot down by Chinese MiGs when they descended to relight a flamed out engine which happened many times.

I had the pleasure to visit with Gimo Yang at his home in Las Vegas prior to his death three years ago. We enjoyed a visit of reminiscing about the old days.

From Gerald E. McIlmoyle

My wife, Patty, and I invited some of the Black Cats to dinner one evening. Patty served beef stroganoff over rice, one of my favorites. After they left, she castigated herself for serving my Chinese students rice. They were real gentlemen though. I didn't notice any unusual responses during the meal, and they ate what she served with relish.

When teaching them something about a U-2 system, I learned early on not to ask, "do you understand?" They always answered "yes" even when they didn't understand. I had learned about 'Face' when stationed in Korea and Japan. I knew from the look in their eyes my explanations were not clear to them. It was important that they understood. The only way get around the 'Face' problem was to take them to the aircraft and ask them to show me. Then, and only then, did I know they knew what I wanted them to know and how to operate that system.

I enjoyed working with all the Black Cats immensely. They were good pilots, but the language barrier was my biggest problem. However, we seemed to get around that, and I was confident they could get the U-2 to do what it was designed to do.

I transferred out of the 4080th SRW before their training was finished, but I was told by Roger Herman they all finished training and were rated Highly Qualified on their Standardization Board Check rides.

From Chris Pocock

The Black Cats? I've met a dozen of them over the years, in Taiwan, the US, and even in mainland China. Their stories were fascinating, and emblematic of the complex web of family and political relationships between the two Chinas.

Some of their personalities were as I expected, some not. "Gimo" Yang was just as described by others; a gregarious former fighter pilot, happy to tell his incredible tales of dodging death over the mainland skies in RF-84s as well as U-2. He was living in retirement in Las Vegas when we met, and no doubt entertaining the croupiers and dealers at the gambling tables there, with his fund of stories.

Colonel Lu was similarly outgoing. He had also made America his home, and was living in Los Angeles when we met. In fact, a whole community of former Taiwan military officers and their families seemed to be living in the Monterey Park area. Colonel Lu was leader of their social organization – and a great enthusiast for country dancing.

"Tiger" Wang was another member of that expatriate community in Los Angeles. A small, mild-mannered man, he was much quieter than Lu or Yang.

So was Mike Hua, quite unlike most generals that I have met, serving or retired. Looking at his studious face beneath the U-2 pressure helmet in an old photo, one could sense that he might have a different future from the usual military flyer. I first met Gen Hua at the Aero Industry Development Center (AIDC) in Taiching, which he commanded. After flying the U-2, his engineering degree led to his key role in developing Taiwan's Indigenous Defense Fighter (IDF), of which he is justly proud. He has written well about that experience, as well as about his fellow Black Cats.

By the time I met them, most of the Black Cats had family connections in North America, or had emigrated themselves there. Why had they left 'The Beautiful Island'? It seemed to me, that the exposure to the English language and American ways during their military careers had created an alternative future pathway that Taiwan could not match. Instead of the US, Johnny Shen chose Canada, where I first met him. But like most of the others, he would return to Taiwan at least once a year.

That option was not open to Jack Chang when I first met him, at a retirement home in McLean, VA where he was a manager. When Taiwan refused to re-admit him and fellow captive, Robin Yeh, after their release from the mainland, the Agency resettled them in the US. Robin made clear his bitterness with the powers-that-be in Taiwan and told me that he would never return to Taiwan permanently.

An adaptation of my 1989 book *Dragon Lady* was released in Chinese in Taiwan, by the publisher of a leading newspaper there. It was the first time that the unfortunate story of Robin and Jack had been publicized in Taiwan. The newspaper ran extracts from the book, and ran a campaign to force the government to invite the two pilots home. The campaign succeeded, and I am proud of my role in gaining proper acknowledgment for these two heroes. I have since met Jack a couple of times at the apartment in Taipei where he now makes home.

I met "Spike" Chuang a couple of times in Taiwan. He told his tales in amusing fashion, and had a mature perspective on his past. After his military career, he had done business with the mainland, and I learned something about the divided loyalties of the Chinese diaspora from him. Spike told me of his reaction, when briefed for the first time of his mission to drop the sensor pods over Lop Nor. Having initially been told nothing about their purpose, for security reasons, he wondered whether they were nuclear weapons. If so, he told me, he would abort the mission. Although (like the others) he was from a Nationalist family, he was proud that China had demonstrated the technical prowess to build The Bomb.

Andy Fan was a good interviewee; excellent recall and modest about his achievements. And I must not forget Mory Tsai, who has been a wonderful host and interlocutor on Taiwan.

And what of Johnny Wang, living quietly in self-imposed exile when I met him in Beijing in 2009? He was the one who defected to the People's Republic by flying a China Airlines 747 to Guangzhou in 1986. We needed an interpreter to converse; Johnny had little need to practice his English skills, which had therefore faded over time. Now retired, he had served for years with China's state airline. The circumstances of the interview were such, that it seemed to me inappropriate, to delve into his past decisions. He is just another strand in that complex web.

Appendix II

ROCAF U-2 Pilots

Yoahua Chih
Huai Chen
Shihchu (Gimo) Yang
Hsichun (Mike) Hua
Taiyu (Tiger) Wang
Nanping (Terry) Li
Chang di (Robin) Yeh
Shichuen (Johnny) Wang
Tehpei (Sonny) Liang
Liyi (Jack) Chang
Chenwen (Pete) Wang
Tseshi (Charlie) Wu
Chingchang (Mickey) Yu
Jenliang (Spike) Chuang
Jaichang (Terry) Liu
Huangdi (Andy) Fan
Hsieh (Billy) Chang
Yenchun Chou
Lungpei (Tom) Hwang
Chihsien (Denny) Hwang
Paowei (David) Lee
Tao (Tom) Wang
Chungli (Johnny) Shen
Chu Chien
Sungchou Chiu
Chen Wei
Chichiang Yee
Shenghsiung (Mory) Tsai

Appendix III

History of the U-2 and the ROC

When the Central Intelligence Agency was established in 1947, no one could predict that in less than a decade that agency would develop a program of overhead reconnaissance primarily to overfly the Soviet Union. It was the responsibility of the military service to fly deep into unfriendly territory during wartime. By the 1950s, the US required strategic intelligence on the Soviet Union and its satellite states. USAF and Navy aircraft had conducted peripheral recon overflights, but the high mortality rate and increased international tension deemed the missions too risky.

The Air Force began developing a high-altitude reconnaissance aircraft capable of deep-penetration missions over the Soviet Union. President Eisenhower feared the loss of such an aircraft deep in Soviet territory would lead to war. Therefore, he authorized the development of a new non-military aircraft, first the U-2 and later the A-12 OXCART. The plan was for the aircraft to be manned by civilians, operated under cover and in the deepest secrecy. At this time, primary responsibility for the new reconnaissance program was assigned to the CIA, with the Air Force providing vital support.

The USAF and Navy tried to acquire aerial photographs over the Soviet Union with the USAF using the Boeing RB-47. At that time the Soviet Union had not completely surrounded its borders with radar; much of the interior of the country also lacked radar coverage. When one RB-47 found a gap in the network, they darted inland quickly to photograph accessible targets. One RB-47 managed to fly 450 miles inland. These intrusions resulted in protests from Moscow but no Soviet military response.

In 1950 the Soviet Union implemented a major change in policy, and air defense units became very aggressive defending their airspace, attacking all aircraft that came near their border. Soviet Union air defense policy became even more aggressive in August 1952 when its reconnaissance aircraft began violating Japanese airspace over Hokkaido, the northernmost Japanese island. On October 7, 1952, Soviet fighters shot down a US RB-29 that flew over Hokkaido. (See *We Served with Honor* by Linda Rios Bromley, James F. Bard Jr. and Frank T. Hayes for a detailed account of this event).

Despite the risks, senior US officials strongly believed that such missions were necessary. The lack of information increased the US determination to secure evidence of Soviet capabilities and reduce the danger of a surprise attack by the Soviet Union. The theory was that the best Soviet interceptor, the MiG17, struggled to reach even 45,000 feet. Initially, the plan was to modify existing aircraft which brought attention to the British twin-engine medium bomber, the Canberra. By this time, the USAF had adopted the bomber version of the Canberra, the Martin Aircraft Company B-57. With reconfigurations such as long high-lift wings, Rolls Royce Avon 109 engines, a single cockpit and an airframe stressed less than standard military specs, the aircraft could possibly reach an altitude as high as 67,000 feet.

In March 1953 a request for proposal was issued for "an aircraft weapon system having operational radius of 1,500 nautical miles and capable of conducting pre- and post-strike reconnaissance missions during daylight." Additional requirements stated the aircraft must have optimum subsonic cruise speed at altitudes of 70,000 feet or higher. A single cockpit for one pilot and capability of carrying up to 700 pounds of reconnaissance equipment was a critical requirement.

By January 1954, three companies, Bell Aircraft Corporation of Buffalo, New York, Fairchild Engine and Airplane Corporation of Hagerstown Maryland and Glenn L. Martin Company of Baltimore had submitted proposals. Word of the competition for the new reconnaissance aircraft reached another manufacturer in the industry. Lockheed Aircraft Corporation then submitted an unsolicited design. Lockheed's design incorporated some non-standard design philosophy, such as the elimination of landing gear, disregard of the military specifications and the use of very low load factors.

Lockheed's senior officials approved the proposal and early in 1954, the company's best aircraft designer, Clarence (Kelly) Johnson, began working on the project known as CL-282. Johnson was already recognized as one of the world's leading aeronautical engineers, and had to his credit the P-38, P-80, F-104 and Constellation. His design was based upon the fuselage of the F-104 but incorporated a sailplane wing. To save weight and increase the aircraft's altitude, Johnson stressed the airframe to only 2.5 units of gravity (G's) instead of the military specs of 5.33 G's. His selection for the power plant was the General Electric 173/GE-3 non-afterburning turbojet engine with 9,300 pounds of thrust. The wings and tail were detachable. One of the most significant features was the landing gear; Johnson proposed two skis and a reinforced belly rib for landing. A wheeled dolly to be jettisoned on takeoff would enable the aircraft to taxi. Other unusual features were: an unpressurized cockpit, a 15-cubic foot payload area to accommodate 600 pounds of sensors, maximum altitude of 70,000 feet and range of 2,000 miles.

In March 1954, Kelly Johnson submitted the CL-282 design to members of the Office of Development Planning at the Pentagon. Subsequently, Lockheed was requested to submit a specific proposal. In April, Johnson made a presentation of the CL-282 design which included construction and maintenance of 30 aircraft to senior Pentagon officials. Following the presentation, Johnson remarked that civilian officials were very interested in his design but the generals were less than enthusiastic. The CL-282 design presentation was conducted for General Curtis E. LeMay, CINC Strategic Air Command. Halfway through the presentation, LeMay told the briefers in his customary brusk manner, "if I want high altitude photographs, I'll put cameras in the B-36 bomber. I'm not at all interested in a plane with no wheels or guns. This is a total waste of my time."

In June 1954, Lockheed received a letter from the Air Force officially rejecting CL-282 because it had only one engine and its design was too radical. The Air Force was already committed to the modification of the Martin B-57. Undaunted, Lockheed continued to work on the CL-282 and began seeking new sources of support for the aircraft.

Though the Air Force's uniformed hierarchy favored the Bell and Martin aircraft, some senior civilian officials continued to support the Lockheed design. Trevor Gardner, Special Assistant for Research and Development to Air Force Secretary Harold Talbot, had countless contacts in west coast aeronautical circles. Prior to his assignment in Washington, Gardner headed the Hycon Manufacturing Company, makers of aerial cameras. He attended Kelly Johnson's presentation to the Pentagon and believed it showed the most promise for reconnaissance of the Soviet Union.

Gardner envisioned CL-282 as primarily a collector of strategic rather than tactical intelligence. He tried to interest Gen LeMay in the Lockheed design, but LeMay had already expressed disinterest in unarmed aircraft. Gardner decided to seek CIA support for the Lockheed design. At the time, the Agency's involvement was limited to an advisory capacity to the Air Force regarding the launch of camera-carrying balloons over hostile territory. In May 1954 Gardner met with Philip Strong, Chief of Operations Staff and Office of Scientific Intelligence at the CIA. Strong was supportive of the Lockheed reconnaissance aircraft and considered it to be the best of those proposals submitted. Gardner asked Strong if the CIA would be interested in such an aircraft. Strong promised to present the Lockheed design to the Agency's newly hired Special Assistant for Planning and Coordination, Richard Bissell. Preoccupied with a number of ongoing Agency operations, Bissell agreed the plan had merit. He suggested that Strong enlist the help of some well recognized scientists for advice and recommendations.

Strong continued to seek support for high altitude overflight. In May 1954 Strong persuaded DCI Allen W. Dulles to ask the Air Force to take the initiative for approval of an overflight of the Soviet guided missile test range at Kapustin Yar. CIA and Air Force officials discussed the idea on several occasions, but the Air Force rejected it in October 1954. Dulles was supportive of the Air Force overflight of the Soviet Union, but he did not want the CIA to be involved in a project designated for the military as Lockheed CL-282 had been. Primarily Dulles favored the traditional form of espionage, relying on agents rather than technology.

By the summer of 1954, though Lockheed's design had strong support from Air Force civilian and CIA officials, decision makers at those agencies were not as convinced. To add credibility to Kelly Johnson's design, support from prominent scientists was critical. The Beacon Hill Study Group, a collection of recognized experts who met in Boston, began seeking information about targets behind the Iron Curtain at the request of Strategic Air Command. During January and February 1952, the group traveled every weekend to airbases, laboratories and corporations for briefings on cutting edge technology and projects. They were especially interested in new approaches to aerial reconnaissance. One of the most radical proposals was an 'invisible' almost flat-shaped airship with non-reflective coating. The designers predicted it could cruise to an altitude of 90,000 feet along the borders of the Soviet Union at slow speed while operating a large lens to photograph targets. However, this design had no support.

Following their travels and briefings, the Beacon Hill Study Group returned to Boston and wrote a lengthy report which advocated radical approaches to acquire intelligence. The report covered radar, radio and photographic surveillance. One of the key recommendations called for the development of high altitude reconnaissance aircraft. The Air Force had not implemented the recommendations of the Beacon Hill Report until President Dwight Eisenhower was elected in January 1953. Almost immediately, he expressed dissatisfaction with the intelligence estimates of Soviet capabilities and the lack of reconnaissance on the Soviet Bloc. The President as well as US political and military leaders believed the Soviet Union was a dangerous opponent. Most alarming was the progress of the Soviets in the area of nuclear weapons. High ranking officials viewed the Soviet Union as a threat to peace and world order.

In the spring of 1953, a Top Secret study pointed out the vulnerability of US SAC bases to a surprise attack by Soviet long range bombers. An American military attaché sighted a new Soviet intercontinental bomber at an airfield south of Moscow. The aircraft designated

Bison by NATO appeared to be a native Soviet design which surprised US intelligence experts and was reported to pose a significant threat to the US.

By July 1953 the Air Force had established the Intelligence Systems Panel (ISP) consisting of several experts from the Beacon Hill Study Group, including participation from the CIA. When the ISP met in August 1953, Philip Strong informed the panel members the best intelligence available on the Soviet Union's interior was photography taken by the German Luftwaffe during the Second World War, but many vital regions were not included.

A number of Air Force reconnaissance projects were discussed: new cameras, reconnaissance balloons, satellites and multiple sensors for use in existing aircraft. Another big topic was the search for a new high altitude reconnaissance aircraft. The variety of programs discussed were products of the Air Force effort to find a way to collect intelligence on the Soviet Bloc. Some plans were beyond the existing level of technology; others such as camera carrying balloons were feasible but were considered too dangerous due to political consequences.

The CIA's manned overhead reconnaissance program operated from 1954 to 1974 with two extraordinary aircraft, the U-2 and the A-12 OXCART. The program and recon systems that were developed changed the Agency's work and structure in ways that were revolutionary and permanent. The formation of the Directorate of Science and Technology in the 1960s to develop and direct reconnaissance programs is the most obvious legacy of these events.

The struggle between the CIA and the USAF to control the U-2 and A-12 projects exposed problems that beset successor programs. The U-2 was an enormous technological success. Its first flight over the USSR in July 1956 immediately made it the most important source of intelligence on the Soviet Union. However, use of the aircraft against the Soviet target produced continuous tension between program managers and President Eisenhower. Program managers repeatedly urged the president to authorize frequent missions over the Soviet Union. President Eisenhower, cautious of the propriety of invading Soviet airspace, only reluctantly allowed any overflights at all. When Francis Gary Powers' U-2 was shot down over Soviet territory on May 1, 1960, the president prohibited future flights over the USSR.

Bibliography

Davison, Gary Marvin and Barbara E. Reed, *Culture and Customs of Taiwan* Westport, CT: Greenwood Press, 1998.

Fu-En, I., *My Memoirs*: Taipei 104: Taiwan, Li Ching Cultural and Educational Foundation, 2003.

Hua, Mike H., *Lost Black Cats, Story of Two Captured Chinese U-2 Pilots:* Bloomington, IND: Author House, 2005.

Taylor, Jay, *The Generalissimo, Chiang Kai-Shek and the Struggle for Modern China:* Cambridge MA: Harvard University Press, 2009.

Tsai, Yung Pang, *Through The Eyes of The Night Owl:* Bloomington, IND: Author House, 2009.